Leader's Guide

Leader's Guide

Dr. David R. Grimm

iUniverse, Inc.
New York Bloomington

Doorway to H.O.P.E. Leader's Guide, Second Edition

To request permission, to make a donation, or to contact Help Overcoming Painful Experiences (H.O.P.E.), please write to us at:

Help Overcoming Painful Experiences (H.O.P.E.)
P.O. Box 24419
Belleville, IL 62223

Or for more information about us, visit our website at:

helpovercomingpainfulexperiences.org

iUniverse books may be ordered through booksellers or by contacting:

iUniverse
1663 Liberty Drive
Bloomington, IN 47403
www.iuniverse.com
1-800-Authors (1-800-288-4677)

ISBN: 978-0-595-40306-6 (sc)
ISBN: 978-0-595-84682-5 (ebk)

Printed in the United States of America

iUniverse rev. date: 05/14/2010

Dedication

This book and program are dedicated to five people: my wife Tiffany Grimm, our two sons Jonah and Jacob, Bob Poskitt and Pastor Alan Owens. My wife Tiffany is the love of my life and my best friend. Never was a more beautiful woman ever created and I would simply be incomplete without her. Our two sons Jonah and Jacob are the very faces of God's love and goodness in my life. I am extremely proud of both of them and honored to be their father. I hope and pray that I can always be the father they need me to be by pointing them to The Cross during both the enjoyable and painful experiences in their lives. Bob Poskitt, my original mentor, who sadly passed away in 2007, is the one who made all this possible. All my books and this entire ministry are all the result of his godly influence in my life. This ministry will forever by a living memorial to him and his passion to help the hurting. Pastor Alan Owens is my continuing mentor. As mentors, both Bob and Alan have given me invaluable direction and inspiration in my walk with Jesus and my experience with this ministry.

Table of Contents

Acknowledgements

This book, program and organization have been decades in the making because they are all the direct result of my life experiences. There are many, many people who have influenced my life in such a way as to contribute to their development and this is my attempt to thank them.

I am most grateful to my loving wife, Tiffany, for enabling me to do all that I do. Thank you for believing in me to accomplish God's calling on my life. Your encouragement and support empowered me to succeed in writing this material. I also wish to thank you for all your editorial contributions to this book and all the other ways you now serve with me in this organization.

I wish to thank Bob Poskitt, my dear friend and mentor in the support ministry, who sadly passed away in 2007. His Biblical wisdom, love and compassion for men like me who were dealing with emotional pain are what started me on the journey to the place I am today. This book, along with all my books, and this entire ministry are all the result of his godly influence in my life. Without his obedience to God's call on his life, none of this would have ever happened. I will always miss you, but I look forward to seeing you again some day.

I am grateful to Pastor Joe Boerman for giving me permission to incorporate many of his wise and practical teachings in my writing. I am grateful to Pastor Alan Owens for being my mentor and source of encouragement in this area. I also wish to thank both pastors for their wisdom, direction, inspiration, counsel and friendship.

To all the Grimm family members, both by birth and by marriage, I am thankful for your love, acceptance and support. I will also be forever grateful for being Uncle Buck to all of you!

In addition, I wish to thank my brother, Robert Grimm, for creating such a beautiful cover for the book. By capturing the exact look and message I sought for this book to portray, your talents as a graphic designer shine as second to none. I am also thankful to his wife, Karen, for her outstanding graphic designs and her support of this organization. The expertise, support and generosity we receive from both of you are a true blessing.

To my other brothers Wayne and Jim Grimm, and my sister Julie Thompson, I also thank you for your support and partnership in this organization. To my father James Grimm, I thank you for just being my father. I also thank you for allowing me to be who I am by providing the affirmation that I can do what I am called to do.

To all the Wilson family members, both by birth and by marriage, I am indebted to all of you for your love and acceptance. You never judged me and have received me as one of your own. I thank you for that, and for always being there to support us.

To my Aunt and Uncle Tom and Fran Smith (and Kevin) and to my Aunt Sharon Smith, I thank you for all your support in my life (and to Tom for his direction with our organization and the publishing of these materials).

To Fernando Ortega, I wish to thank you for your music. There is something truly special about your songs and the way they touch me. Your music has been an inspiration to me and God used it to help me write our programs (which I listened to every time I wrote). So in addition to all the beautiful music you have composed, you also helped compose our programs. Because of this you are an important part of our ministry.

I am grateful to Todd Arvidson for mentoring me in how to lead a support group. I also thank you for showing me how to create and utilize a Spiritual and Emotional Blueprint. To Dave Gillaspie, Matt Smith and Ricky White, I wish to thank you both for all the generosity and expertise that have been a blessing to this organization. To Pat Mathis and Philip Speicher, I thank you for all your legal assistance. To Mary Ann Nold, I thank you for all your accounting support. To Dr. George Harton, I am thankful for your encouragement and your review of this book. Your insight was greatly appreciated and led to the creation and publishing of the 2nd Edition.

I wish to thank the original core group within H.O.P.E.: Steve Christian, Diane DeJong, Wendie Gates, Shelly Goodman, Yvonne Harter, Rosetta Klein, Doug Saesan, Kathy Saesan, Robin Simmonds and Bonnie Willms. I will always be grateful for the family we have become.

To small group members Steve and Tracy Kemmet, Grace and Eric Kurtz, Larry and Carol Lucas, Alan and Susan Owens, Beth Rivelli, Lori Rosenberry and Scott and Colette Schaffer, I am grateful for the friendship, support and encouragement I have received from all of you.

I am also grateful for the wisdom, support and friendship I have received from many other godly men in my life, including Lloyd Biddle, Jeff Brown, Jay Brubaker, Scott Compton, Bulus Galadima, Pastor Brian Henry, Doug Leafblad, Dave Pfeifer, Jeff Rector, Ken Schroeder, Dick Smith, Jim Stewart, Bill Stinchcomb and Jerry Winslow.

There are many other dear friends who have stood by me and helped me over the years and to whom I will be eternally grateful, including Jonathan and Kim Bobby, Jeff and Jamie Butler, Dave and Laura Gore, Tim and Cathy Hasenstab (and family), Kenny Johnson, Toby and Wendy Mueller and Ronnie and Rhonda Holley-Shanks.

There are many other friends who have supported me in many ways throughout my life, including Michael and Candi Abella, the Bobby family, Dr. Pete and Charmayne Brust, Tom and Julie Burckhardt, Don Canter, Juli Chaffee, Joe and Mary Consorti, Lee Davis, Tim and Janine Dolinka, John and Charisse DuBois, Greg Eitzenhefer, Rick Fattore, John Girlandis, Pastor Jeff Gokee, Mark Goldsmith, Pastor Brian Gorman, Eric and Kelly Gregori, Dr. John Hassell, Don Jillson, Rita Joyce, Dan Kassebaum, Dr. David Lafrenz, Rev. and Pastor Steve and Melanie Lane, Dr. Paul Legaard, Roy LeGrand, John and Cynthia Lovell, Dr. Joan Lunney, Dr. John Martinko, Ron McCarthy, Pastor Eric Meyer, Dr. Michael Misfeldt, Pete Moberg, Gary Morgan, Chudy Nduaka, Brian Norton, Brian Orlet, David and Jayne Orlet, Jim Orlet, Kelvin Oxendine, Richard and Marian Queen, Pastor Tim Ritzel, Sixto Robles, David Rothbard, David Sefcik, Fred and Jennifer Seiferth, Gordon and Cherisse Selley, Chris Southworth, Dr. Brian Spear, Pastor Mike Stephens, Owen and Linda Towles (and family), Greg Turner, Pastor Jamie Wamsley, Jeff Warren, Jim Woodard and Mike Yeager. To all of you, all I can say is thank you.

Finally, at the risk of stating the obvious, I wish to thank my Lord and Savior Jesus Christ. I thank You for dying for me and giving me a hope and future, both here on earth and eternally. I thank You for my life. I thank You for my wife and sons. I thank You for not leaving me where I was. I thank You for loving me and caring about me. I thank You for Your healing and restoring power. I thank You for allowing all the difficult times and pain I experienced so that You could use them to teach me more about You and to mold me into who I am. I thank You for going to such great lengths to draw me close to You and establish our relationship. I thank You that You are not finished with me and there are more exciting things yet to come. I thank You for leading me on this journey and speaking to me so clearly about the creation of H.O.P.E. and the development of our program. Finally, I thank You for somehow considering me worthy of this calling on my life. I only hope You are proud of me and the way I responded to Your call.

The History of Help Overcoming Painful Experiences (H.O.P.E.)

I started Help Overcoming Painful Experiences (H.O.P.E.) in 2002 in response to God's calling on my life to minister to those who are hurting. The name was chosen as an acrostic to reflect what we represent; Help Overcoming Painful Experiences. My passion in this area comes from my own experiences with emotional pain (involving decades of anger and depression) and the desire to give back to others the Biblically based support and help I have received.

I am particularly grateful to Bob Poskitt, who befriended me during my divorce proceedings in 1996 (the lowest time in my life). In addition to my divorce, I experienced a series of painful events that year (further described in this book) that caused me to struggle mightily with my anger and depression. As I had previously done in my life, I again made many unhealthy choices and I wanted to give up and end it all. I wasted too much time being mad at God and felt as if He abandoned me. I would read the Bible, put it down, and then ask God why all the promises I had just read held true for everyone but me.

But during this difficult time, Bob assisted me and other men in my situation by mirroring Jesus as he wisely, diligently, truthfully and lovingly helped me to overcome decades of emotional pain. I found a safe place where I could express my true feelings and receive the support of others who knew what it felt like to be me. That support, combined with Bob replacing the lies in my mind with the truth of God's Word, resulted in a change taking place inside me. It definitely did not happen overnight, but this change was initiated slowly and steadily. I started to see my situation in a different light, the light of God's truth. Bob's godly influence in my life is the primary reason that I am still here today because his group literally changed my life.

One of the most impactful things I learned during this time was how much God truly cares about me. God actually went to some very specific and very amazing lengths to make that extremely clear to me. Not only that, I also began to see that there was actually a reason why all this pain came into my life. God had a plan. The plan included not getting angry about my pain, or getting depressed about it, but learning how to embrace it and deal with it head on in a positive, truthful and healthy way. God's plan began to unfold over the next several years, which included meeting and marrying my wife Tiffany, followed by us moving to the Chicago area in 2001.

One aspect of God's plan involved teaching me through my experiences that He is in the business of change. God also taught me that He never wastes a hurt and that our greatest pain can produce our greatest opportunities to minster (if we will only allow God to work His plan in our lives). I learned that as a result of my experiences, opportunities were created to minister to others who were hurting. I had earned the right to be heard. Therefore, it was through my own experiences with emotional pain, combined with my involvement in a Christ-centered support group, that the Lord prepared me for service in this area.

H.O.P.E. began as an attempt to meet the needs of people who were struggling with painful experiences in my church and in my community. As our ministry grew, God impressed upon me the need to more aggressively promote H.O.P.E. in a way that can penetrate and transform our entire world. I followed

God's calling and direction and incorporated H.O.P.E. as a non-profit organization in the state of Illinois in 2005, of which I am the CEO. I continued to follow God's calling in my life to "do more" and created the program and the Three Level Transformation Model (further described in that section of this book) we now use in H.O.P.E. In 2006, I published the two primary books in our program, *Doorway to H.O.P.E.* and *Names of H.O.P.E.* These books were written using everything I have learned from my mentor Bob Poskitt, everything I have learned from my experiences and a number of other principles from God's Word that I have learned along the way. They were designed as a systematic and extensive Bible study through God's principles and purpose for pain, the truth of His character in the midst of pain, how He can transform us through our pain and how He can empower us to fulfill our purpose in life.

As a result, we believe our program is unique. We are not a 12 Step Program, a recovery program or counseling. Rather, we intentionally created a program that focuses on our purpose; transformation. (Our purpose statement is further described in **The Purpose of H.O.P.E.** section of this book.)

Continuing to follow God's calling to grow and reach more people who are lost and hurting, we received our 501c3 tax exempt status as a non-profit organization in 2007. In 2008, I published a companion book for our program called *The Spiritual & Emotional Coach's Guide*, which was designed to empower the Spiritual and Emotional Coaches (SPECs) our members utilize in our program. We also want to equip those people with the knowledge needed to effectively function as a SPEC, thereby helping them help others. People who have been through our program often make ideal SPECs.

In 2009, we hosted our first conference which has quickly become one of our primary areas of emphasis and has since been incorporated into our threefold vision. This vision is further described in **The Purpose of H.O.P.E.** section of this book and includes hosting conferences, developing H.O.P.E. Centers, and developing affiliated locations. Through all these efforts in our vision we have developed a strong calling to reach those who are currently outside the church.

At the time of this writing, we are continuing to aggressively pursue the purpose and vision God has birthed in us. We are standing in faith that what God started in H.O.P.E., He will bring to completion and fulfillment for the glory of His Name.

Sincerely,
Dr. David R. Grimm
CEO, Founder and Author
Help Overcoming Painful Experiences

The Premise of H.O.P.E.

In case you have not noticed, there are countless people hurting today. The reason is because life hurts. It hurts all of us. No one is immune from the pain of life. The statistics for people struggling with the pain of things like divorce, financial troubles, depression, anxiety, guilt, resentment, abuse of all kinds, loss of all kinds, addictions of all kinds, people living without purpose and meaning, etc., are staggering. Then, when you add in the damaging ways that people are trying to cope with their pain, the problems escalate even further.

The fact is we all turn to something to help us cope. And in my opinion, because we have not done enough to equip people to handle the pain of life, they end up turning to the devil's playground for ways to cope with their pain, which, of course, the devil loves. We end up playing right into his hands. The devil then uses our pain and our attempts to cope with our pain to devour and destroy our lives. And he has been getting away with this destruction of lives for far too long without enough resistance. In case you are unaware, that means we are in danger of allowing our society to collapse in spiritual and emotional defeat. That is just wrong!

But all of this is what we seek to change through H.O.P.E. We purposed to start a revolution, a revolution that goes beyond a bandage for the symptoms to focusing on curing the disease, a revolution that goes beyond recovery as an endpoint to focusing on transformation. To be honest, we are not interested in helping anyone recover. Recovery implies that you got back to the point you were prior to experiencing some difficulty. We want our members to go beyond where they have ever been before. So rather than focus on recovery, we were founded on the principle of transformation.

Therefore, we do not focus on helping people overcome their pain just so they can feel better, we empower our members to go further and fulfill their God-ordained purpose in life. We believe that if you free people from their emotional bondage, they will be able to do just that. If you do not help free them first, we do not believe they will ever fully reach God's proper destination.

To help people accomplish this, we created the program and the Three Level Transformation Model we now use in H.O.P.E. The two primary books in our program, *Doorway to H.O.P.E.* and *Names of H.O.P.E.* were written as a systematic and extensive Bible study through God's principles and purpose for pain, the truth of His character in the midst of pain, how He can transform us through our pain and how He can empower us to fulfill our purpose in life. As a result, we believe our program is unique. We are not a 12 Step Program, a recovery program or counseling. Rather, we intentionally created a program that focuses on transformation.

As we teach these principles in our program, we walk with our members through their pain, we help them develop a healthy support network and we help them make the changes that God is prompting them to make. We can accomplish this because our Three Level Transformation Model (further described in that section of this book) is designed to provide long term truth, instruction, guidance, encouragement, support, and spiritual and emotional growth (all in a healthy environment). We believe that God's process of transformation takes time, which is why we developed the model we use. We believe it would be wrong to offer short term programs as a supposed answer for long term issues. Plus, our goal is to empower people to experience a transformation for their entire life, not just help them deal with their current issues. Therefore, we believe our Three Level Transformation Model is also unique because it is designed to provide for the long haul.

Our program and model do not focus on any specific topics. We believe that it does not matter what the source of your pain is because God's principles always apply. Therefore, we have a broad target that includes people struggling with issues like divorce, depression, anxiety, abuse, illness, loss (loved ones, finances, hopes and dreams), discouragement, frustration, anger, addictions, guilt, living a life without purpose and meaning, etc.

Regardless of the issue, we assist those in need and apply God's truth to painful experiences. We expose the lies that hold people in bondage to their pain and replace them with the truth of God's Word. As one of our founding verses says in John 8:32, *"...you shall know the truth, and the truth shall make you free"* (NASV). We shine the light of truth into difficult situations and show how changing our thought process to one like God's can free us and transform our attitudes, behaviors and understanding of God during painful times in life. As another one of our founding verses says in Romans 12:2, *"And do not be conformed to this world, but be transformed by the renewing of your mind, that you may prove what the will of God is, that which is good and acceptable and perfect"* (NASV). We help people stop embracing and fellowshipping with their pain and the lies, and help them start embracing and fellowshipping with Jesus Christ and the truth.

Another foundation of our ministry is that our leaders are people who have been there, too. H.O.P.E. members ultimately make ideal leaders because they know and understand. So as a ministry, we are there to pass along the same support we have received to others who are hurting. As Paul wrote in 2 Corinthians 1:3-5 (another one of our foundational Scriptures), *"Blessed be the God and Father of our Lord Jesus Christ, the Father of mercies and God of all comfort; who comforts us in all our afflictions so that we may be able to comfort those who are in any affliction with the comfort with which we ourselves are comforted by God. For just as the sufferings of Christ are ours in abundance, so also our comfort is abundant through Christ"* (NASV).

In 2009, we hosted our first conference which has quickly become one of our primary areas of emphasis and has since been incorporated into our threefold vision. This vision is further described in **The Purpose of H.O.P.E.** section of this book and includes hosting our *A Revolution of H.O.P.E.* conferences, developing H.O.P.E. Centers, and developing affiliated locations.

Through all of these efforts, we have developed a strong calling to reach those who are currently outside the church. Therefore, we are planning to do things a little differently so we can more effectively integrate our ministry into our communities and change the face of emotional and spiritual health around the globe.

We hope and pray that since you have begun reading his book, you will take the next step and pursue a healthy, vibrant and life-changing relationship with Jesus Christ. We hope that you will investigate, pursue and ultimately accept God's unique and eternal perspective on your painful experiences and allow Him to reveal Himself to you through His Names and His truth. God can and will use your trials and pain to transform you and bring you to a better place because God is in the business of change. Your past and your present are not the deciding factors in your future; Jesus Christ is. We hope that you allow Him to work His transformation process in you and trust that His ways and plan are best.

No matter what you have been through in the past, what you are going through in the present, or what you will go through in the future, the truth is that nothing can separate you from the love of God in Christ Jesus. Since our relationship with the Lord Jesus is the only thing we will carry into eternity, He places paramount importance on this relationship. Therefore, He will go to any length to develop, strengthen and mature that relationship with each and every one of us. One of the most important ways God chooses to do this is through pain and suffering. There seems to be no other way to effectively teach us certain things about Him and to mold our character and image to one that more reflects His. And believe it or not, the truth is that God does all this because He wants to draw us closer to Him, because He wants to have a deeper relationship with us. God wants all this because He loves us unconditionally, so much so that He sent His only son Jesus to die for us.

Not only is God in the business of change, but He is also in the business of miracles. In Christ, there are no hopeless situations, only those who have grown hopeless about their situation. There is an enormous difference between those two statements. To resurrect hope, we point people to the God of hope. There is no one and no situation too far gone that God cannot heal and restore, including you and your pain. If you allow God to work in your life according to His ways and plans, He will provide for all of your spiritual, emotional and physical needs as He heals and restores you. If you submit your life and ways to God, no matter how much pain you are experiencing, He will never leave you to endure it alone and He will always clear a path of healing for you, even if it requires a miracle.

No matter how frightening it may seem to take the next step, we have God's promise that He will guide us to the end and never quit on us. As Philippians 1:6 says, "*...being confident of this, that He who began a good work in you will carry it on to completion until the day of Christ Jesus.*" God will be there for you every step of the way to bring you to completion. You have His Word on it, and you will never find a better guarantee than that. So please join with us who have taken this step and are now enjoying the benefits of a transformed life. You will not regret it.

The Purpose of H.O.P.E.

H.O.P.E. is a 501c3 non-profit organization whose **Purpose** is to help people experience a life transformation through their emotional pain so they can live the purpose-filled, victorious life God intended and designed them to live. We exist to set people free from emotional bondage and empower them to live a transformed life by directing them to the healing and restorative power of Jesus Christ. We are not a recovery group, we are not a 12 Step Program and we are not counseling. We are a transformation ministry.

To accomplish our purpose, our program was designed to help people 1) resurrect hope, 2) overcome emotional pain from a variety of issues, 3) build a safe and healthy support network, 4) comprehend the truths about God in the midst of pain while exposing and replacing lies, and 5) experience a life transformation through the healing and restorative power of Jesus Christ.

Our program is a Bible study format that was designed for those in pain. The program clearly and systematically teaches God's principles and purpose for pain, His character and how He relates to us through our pain and how He can transform us through our pain, all the while exposing the lies that hold us in bondage in our pain and replacing them with the truth of God's Word.

Through our program we provide a safe place to work through the emotional issues that hinder us from fully embracing God, others, and life with enthusiasm. As we do this, we do not focus on any specific topics. We believe that it does not matter what the source of your pain is, because God's principles always apply. So we apply God's principles to the pain of issues like divorce, anger, guilt, anxiety, depression, abuse, illness, loss (loved ones, finances, hopes and dreams), addictions, discouragement, frustration, living without purpose and meaning, etc.

Because God's process of transformation takes time, our Three Level Transformation Model is designed to support our members for the long term. Our goal is to empower people to experience a transformation for their entire life, not just help them deal with their current issues.

But our program is not our only approach to helping people live a transformed life; we actually have a threefold approach to our **Vision** to impact communities everywhere. First, we perform conferences in venues throughout the country that are designed to minister to people on a larger scale and generate interest in our ministry in that location. Our conferences focus on uplifting worship, prayer support, and messages developed to share the truth about God's principles and purpose for pain, to answer the question, "Does God really care?", to present God as Restorer, to help people overcome discouragement, and to address the truth about forgiveness.

Second, we plan to develop H.O.P.E. Centers around the country that not only provide our program and model, but also provide additional services/programs to meet the specific needs of the hurting within their local community. Our goal is to develop H.O.P.E. Centers in every state in our country (and eventually around the world).

Third, we develop affiliated locations that offer our program in existing locations like (but not limited to): churches, businesses, schools, prisons, hospitals, health centers, rehabilitation centers, other organizations, etc. These affiliated locations would be supported locally by the H.O.P.E. Centers. Regardless of the location, we can provide the materials, training and support needed to empower them to successfully reproduce our model and impact their community for Jesus Christ.

Through all of these efforts, we have a strong calling to reach those who are currently outside the church. Therefore, we are planning to do things a little differently so we can more effectively integrate our ministry into our communities and change the face of emotional and spiritual health around the globe. We are not going to sit idly and allow hell to devour and destroy any more lives using the weapon of emotional pain. We are not going to allow our society to crumble in spiritual and emotional defeat. We are taking back the spiritual and emotional health that the devil has stolen from countless people and empowering them to live a transformed life.

But in order to accomplish our purpose and vision, we need your support. So please consider joining us by visiting our website (helpovercomingpainfulexperiences.org) and making a tax-deductible donation to our efforts.

H.O.P.E. Testimonials

"H.O.P.E. has changed my life. I remember the night I said I had learned to like myself. That was a totally foreign concept to me, but it had happened. It changed my whole way of thinking."
(Shelly G.)

"H.O.P.E. has taught me that it's all about God and not about me. God is God and I am not. Now, instead of asking 'Why is this happening to me?' I now ask, 'Why is this happening for me.'"
(Steve C.)

"Before coming to H.O.P.E., I was horribly depressed and very angry. I felt lost. I desperately wanted to belong, to be part of a family. But H.O.P.E. has changed all that. I finally have what I've been longing for, people who love me and care about me and miss me if I'm gone. I have a family! I have a family to support and encourage me on life's journey. Instead of desperately wanting to belong, I now desperately want to be used by God to help others know that there is hope."
(Wendie G.)

"I learned that H.O.P.E. was a safe place where people accepted you for who you are. It helped me not be afraid to talk to people. I learned that God wanted me, He loves me unconditionally, and He has a plan for my life."
(Adult H.O.P.E. group member who requested anonymity)

"H.O.P.E. is not the closing of your eyes to the difficulty, the risk or the failure; it's a trust that if I fail now I shall not fail forever and if I'm hurt I shall be healed. It's a trust that God is good all the time, love is powerful, and the future is full of promises."
(Adult H.O.P.E. group member who requested anonymity)

"I would sum up H.O.P.E. as a family, a body of people gathered to heal."
(Eric N.)

"I am overjoyed about H.O.P.E. because H.O.P.E. is a message that can reach the masses. H.O.P.E. is an answer for the hopeless. H.O.P.E. is a place where you can know and understand that God cares."
(Marie N.)

"H.O.P.E. is an awesome vision that all of us just need because we're all hurting."
(Charlie L.)

"As a man, I can come in and share my painful experiences and my wounds and my brothers and sisters in H.O.P.E. will validate those feelings, validate what I'm going through. Things that Satan would love for us to keep in the darkness can be brought out into the light where God can begin healing them. And you can totally feel the experience in that group."
(Trevor M.)

H.O.P.E. Three Level Transformation Model

Our transformation model consists of three levels. We use a three level model for our groups because we believe that God's process of transformation takes time. Therefore, our model is designed to provide long term truth, instruction, guidance, encouragement, support, and spiritual and emotional growth (all in a healthy environment). We provide long term programs to meet the needs of long term emotional issues. Plus, we want to empower people to experience a transformation for their entire life, not just help them deal with their current issues.

Our model also arose from our belief that our emotional issues result from underlying spiritual needs. Emotional health and spiritual health are entwined; they cannot be separated. So we believe that by addressing spiritual needs you can successfully enable transformation that produces emotional wholeness and healing. In this way, we believe we are appropriately addressing the disease and not just the symptoms.

H.O.P.E. groups generally meet once a week for one and a half to two hours. Regardless of which level a member is in, that time is roughly divided in half between the lesson and **Checking In** (discussed further in Lesson 1). The following provides an overview of each level of our model.

1. **Level 1**: This is the central entry point into our program. This group is always "open" for new members, so it allows us to have a group that someone can join on any given day. We use the *Doorway to H.O.P.E.* book in this level, which focuses on the **Three Truths About Life**. These truths are used as encouragement for accepting and beginning God's process of transformation. The lessons are team-taught and presented in a classroom setting. The first half of the time is devoted to presenting the lesson, while the second half of the time is used to break into smaller groups to allow for **Checking In** (discussed further in Lesson 1). Each smaller group has a group leader from the ministry.

   In addition to having a group that is always "open" for new members to join, we have found two more reasons why there is a need for this group. First, many people who come to us are not ready to commit to a program like ours because they are not ready to ask for help and fully surrender their issues and needs to the Lord. Statistics show that most people who come to a program like this require at least six weeks attendance before they decide to work on changing their life. We have actually seen this period take longer, so in writing this program I decided to double the six week "warm up" period and made this program 12 lessons long. At the completion of each Level 1 program, we simply repeat it for the next group of new members.

   This level is designed to resurrect hope, expose needs and lies, tear down barriers to making healthy changes and "wet appetites" for experiencing how God can transform us through our pain, which can be acted upon by entering a Level 2 small group.

2. **Level 2**: These small groups are "closed" and comprised of members who have completed Level 1. Often these groups have already developed from among the members of the smaller groups used for **Checking In** during Level 1. Following this format, we have witnessed stronger bonds created

and a greater level of acceptance within the group members. We also believe that using small groups allows for more individual and personal attention during the **Checking In** time.

These groups follow the book, *Names of H.O.P.E.*, which is a more comprehensive Bible study focused on God's principles and purpose for pain using Names of God that meet the needs of people encountering painful experiences. Each lesson relates one of God's Names to His principles and purpose for pain, the truth of His character in the midst of pain, how He can transform us through our pain and how He can empower us to fulfill our purpose in life. The level can take nine months or more to complete.

Each group leader presents the lessons in the small group, as opposed to having one person present the material for the lesson in a large group setting and then having members divide up into their smaller groups. In addition to a group leader, we also suggest having a co-leader. This is a practical way for others to learn the "ins and outs" of leading a small group. It helps prevent group cancellation, too, if at least one leader can always be present.

3. **Level 3**: These groups generally still follow a small group format, but are more flexible. The purpose of these groups is to capitalize on the small group momentum already generated in Level 2 and enable long-term involvement in God's process of transformation. They are more topic-specific and provide further support and teaching in areas of need that arise in the Level 2 groups. Example topics in Level 3 groups include:

    a. Evangelism
    b. Telling your story
    c. Spiritual formation and growth
    d. Spiritual gifts and service
    e. Visioneering (a book and concept created by Pastor Andy Stanley) and other similar studies designed to encourage, equip and empower members to pursue and live the vision/dream God has given them
    f. Studies focused on particular topics/areas of need

    Regardless of the topic, all the groups in Level 3 are designed to provide continuing opportunities for spiritual growth and long-term involvement in God's process of transformation. Depending on the group, we either use purchased materials or materials that we have written.

Depending on the location and the issues of our members, our decision on whether or not to use gender-specific or topic-specific groups in our levels has been varied. Our program works very well for the issues our members have encountered even if some of the people in a group are there for entirely different reasons. However, and as we have sometimes experienced, one could easily envision some topics that would be better suited to be discussed in a gender-specific group. Or, if there are a number of members there for the same issue, it might be convenient to have a group specific to that topic. So when forming groups, our only advice is to use discretion as necessary and use common sense for maintaining a safe environment in your location.

Finally, the transforming power of our groups can be clearly seen when one considers the various levels that any small group can reach. There are five levels of small groups that have been described. The five levels are:

1. **Cliché** – superficial, patented, non-personal, rehearsed responses.

2. **Ideas and Facts** – sharing of personal statistics and information.
3. **Ideas and Opinions** – sharing becomes more honest and more personal to include ideas and opinions.
4. **Feelings** – honest sharing of feelings.
5. **Peak** – honest sharing of insights, members are teachable, they invite input and they receive feedback well, there is full trust of others and things are done and said with the appropriate attitude and motives within a loving, truthful and honest community.

In a typical small group setting, it takes 9-18 months to attain the level of **Feelings** and 18-24 months to achieve the level of **Peak**. But we have consistently experienced that our H.O.P.E. small groups can start at the **Feelings** level and arrive at the **Peak** level in only a few weeks. Therefore, we strongly suggest that our format for small groups be followed in order for your members to also experience the wonderful transforming power of the H.O.P.E. program.

Guidelines for *Doorway to H.O.P.E.* Small Group Leaders

1. Before leading any H.O.P.E. group, we highly recommend going through H.O.P.E. leadership training. This will equip and empower you in your role as a ministry leader. In addition, you will learn about the need to develop a leadership team to successfully run this program. A team of leaders is needed for all levels of our program. So please begin by developing your leadership team and please contact us if you are interested in this training.
2. Before leading a H.O.P.E. group, we also highly recommend reading our **Contract for H.O.P.E. Leaders.** As part of this process, please first read this section and then turn to **Appendix B** and read the **Contract for H.O.P.E. Leaders.** If you agree to this information and the contract, please sign and date both copies. Submit the appropriate one to your H.O.P.E. location leader and keep the other one as a reminder of your commitment. We utilize these contracts to provide accountability for our members and we believe it is worthwhile for our leaders as well. You can simply copy these forms from the book.
3. Adhere strictly to the *Doorway to H.O.P.E.* Guidelines.
4. Generally speaking, we avoid having spouses (or other family members) in the same smaller group during **Checking In**. This is a general rule of thumb, but there are always exceptions. Please us the appropriate discretion when dealing with spouses and other family members attending the program together.
5. Prior to the first meeting, please read all the *Leader's Note* sections in Lesson 1. The *Leader's Note* in the **Checking In** section of Lesson 1 provides direction and information that is extremely helpful for successfully dividing up into smaller groups for **Checking In**. We also suggest reviewing the *Leader's Note* for each lesson prior to presenting that lesson.
6. Prior to Lesson 10, read the *Leader's Note* for this lesson found at the end of the **Truth** section. Lesson 10 includes a special time of fun for the group and you will need to plan ahead for this lesson.
7. Keep the smaller groups for **Checking In** to 6-8 (or possibly 10) people, including the leader and co-leader.
8. Be Punctual. Roughly divide the time in half, giving 45 minutes for the lesson and then 45 minutes for **Checking In**. This program works best when you give equal attention to both the lesson and **Checking In**. We believe this is important because too much talking and not enough of God's truth from the lesson will not allow the program to work effectively.
    a. The lessons were designed with a 45 minute presentation time in mind. If you stick to this timeline, you should be able to maintain the schedule. This is really important when you have multiple groups meeting and children are included. We want to be punctual so everyone can maintain his or her schedules, too.
    b. With 6-8 people in a group, you can allow up to 5 minutes (our Guidelines say 3-5 minutes) for each member to **Check In** and still maintain your schedule. This will also provide equal

and fair treatment for everyone. We recommend stating the time limit clearly each week so members know what to expect. If problems persist in this area, use a timer to enforce the rule (but do so lovingly).

9. We recommend presenting the lesson first and then **Checking In**. This recommendation is based on our personal experiences. This order has been the most effective.
10. Stick to the lesson. The lessons are written in a logical order and each one builds upon the previous one. Therefore, it is important to present the material as it is written.
11. Encourage participation and completion of homework assignments. Ask questions each week to find out how people are doing in this area.
12. Encourage expressions of emotions; let them "get it out", as long as it happens in a way that still maintains a safe environment. The ***Doorway to H.O.P.E.*** **Guidelines** 6 and 7 (found in Lesson 1 and **Appendix A**) address this issue more completely.
13. Be a part of the group. Share along and do not view your interaction as that of a professor and a student. Rather, view it as being another group member who facilitates the discussion and presents the lesson.
14. Be careful not to give advice, or at least not too much. If a situation warrants telling a member what you did in that same situation, make it very clear that you are not telling them what to do. You are only sharing how you handled a particular situation.
15. At the end of this program, all the leaders involved in the group should fill out the **Checklist for Entry into a Level 2 *Names of H.O.P.E.* Small Group** (found in **Appendix C**) and jointly discuss the results for each group member. We have found it important to use the criteria in this checklist to screen members for entry into a Level 2 small group. The Level 2 groups are much more effective when only those who are ready to join one are allowed in.

Doorway to H.O.P.E. Group Overview

Lesson 1

Introduction

Welcome

Leader's Note: At the beginning of Lesson 2 you will find some trivia questions (and answers) to be used as "ice breakers." They are in Lesson 2 because that is the first actual lesson. However, we highly recommend using ice breakers like trivia, jokes or whatever, with regularity throughout the program. When using trivia, we also encourage providing something like candy as a prize for correct answers (and we always bring enough for everyone to enjoy after the trivia). We have found this practice to greatly increase the comfort level of our members.

Please review the *Leader's Note* in the **Checking In** section of this lesson prior to beginning a group as it contains helpful information on forming your groups and the necessity of developing a leadership team for this program.

Leading Question: How many of you came here feeling scared, nervous, apprehensive, anxious or any other uncomfortable emotion?

To begin with, we want to let you know that it is very common to feel scared, nervous or uncomfortable about being here. So we want to applaud you and thank you for having the courage to take the first and arguably most difficult step of your journey. We believe that you will not regret your decision to join us.

By way of introduction, we will spend this first lesson going through the group guidelines and give you a general overview of *Doorway to H.O.P.E.*

Agenda

1. Our Purpose
2. Schedule
3. Group Overview
4. Goals
5. Lessons
6. *Doorway to H.O.P.E.* Guidelines
7. Other Useful Information

Our Purpose

The **purpose** of H.O.P.E. is to help people experience a life transformation through their emotional pain so they can live the purpose-filled, victorious life God intended and designed them to live. We exist to set people free from emotional bondage and empower them to live a transformed life by directing them to the healing and restorative power of Jesus Christ.

We are not a recovery group, we are not a 12 Step Program and we are not counseling. We are a transformation ministry.

To accomplish our purpose, our program was designed to help people 1) resurrect hope, 2) overcome emotional pain from a variety of issues, 3) build a safe and healthy support network, 4) comprehend the truths about God in the midst of pain while exposing and replacing lies, and 5) experience a life transformation through the healing and restorative power of Jesus Christ.

Through our program we provide a safe place to work through the emotional issues that hinder us from fully embracing God, others, and life with enthusiasm. This means we take the issue of creating a safe environment ***very*** seriously. This is a place where you are safe to express your feelings, talk openly and trust that you will not be judged. It is in the opening and sharing of feelings that the underlying problems are truly exposed and then we can work through them. In doing so:

- We are here to help and provide hope because we care.
- We are passionate about helping.
- We can sympathize and empathize.
- We will walk with you through your pain.
- We are here to honor God in all we do as we travel this road together.

We can make these statements because our ministry leadership is based on people who have also been through painful experiences. So we are here to pass along to you the same support that we have received. As it says in 2 Corinthians 1:3-5, "*Blessed be the God and Father of our Lord Jesus Christ, the Father of mercies and God of all comfort; who comforts us in all our afflictions so that we may be able to comfort those who are in any affliction with the comfort with which we ourselves are comforted by God. For just as the sufferings of Christ are ours in abundance, so also our comfort is abundant through Christ*" (NASV).

As we do this, we do not focus on specific topics. We believe that it does not matter what the source of your pain is because God's principles always apply. We apply God's principles to the pain of issues like divorce, anger, guilt, anxiety, depression, abuse, illness, loss (loved ones, hopes, dreams, finances), addictions, discouragement, frustration, living without purpose and meaning, etc. Therefore, we welcome you regardless of the underlying issue that brought you to H.O.P.E.

Our program is a Bible study format that was designed for those in pain. The program clearly and systematically teaches God's principles and purpose for pain, His character and how He relates to us through our pain and how He can transform us through our pain, all the while exposing the lies that hold us in bondage in our pain and replacing them with the truth of God's Word.

We apply God's truth to painful experiences. John 8:32 says, "*Then you will know the truth, and the truth will set you free.*" We shine the light of truth into difficult situations and show how changing our thought process to one like God's can free us and transform our attitudes, behaviors and understanding of God during painful times in life. As it says in Romans 12:2, "*And do not be conformed to this world, but be transformed by the renewing of your mind, that you may prove what the will of God is, that which is good and acceptable and perfect*" (NASV).

Schedule

This program is designed for groups to meet once a week for the 12 Lessons in this book. A typical meeting length would be for one and a half hours (or possibly two hours). When that meeting occurs will depend on the location, so your local leaders will provide you with this information. In some locations, additional meeting time may be added to the schedule. For example, there may be dinner and worship time before the meeting, or additional social time after the meeting. So please refer to your local leaders for the schedule your group will follow.

> *Leaders Note:* Whatever time you choose to meet and schedule you follow, please make it clear to the group. Also, please let your members know when there will be exceptions to your schedule, such as holidays or scheduled breaks.

Group Overview

Because God's process of transformation takes time, we developed a Three Level Transformation Model. Our model is designed to support our members for the long term. Our goal is to empower people to experience a transformation for their entire life, not just help them deal with their current issues.

This book is Level 1 of our model. Groups in this level are always "open" for new members, so new members may join this group on any given meeting day. The lessons are team-taught and presented in a classroom setting. The first half of the time is devoted to presenting the lesson, while the second half of the time is used to break into smaller groups to allow for **Checking In** (discussed further in the section on **The Lessons**). Each smaller group has a group leader from the ministry.

For the next 12 lessons in this program, we will focus heavily on Matthew 5:3, "*Blessed are the poor in spirit, for theirs is the kingdom of heaven.*" However, this verse as it applies to our lessons, could be translated better as, "*Blessed are those who recognize their need for God.*"

Therefore, in this level we will show how all of us have a deep emotional and spiritual need that only God can fill. In order to begin the process of transformation, we must first arrive at this recognized place of need. So this program replaces the lies we have learned about dealing with pain with the truth of God and His Word. When we are hurting, it can be very difficult for us to discern truth from lies. If we believe the lies, we will follow pursuits that leave us broken and empty.

This level is designed to resurrect hope, expose needs and lies, tear down barriers to making healthy changes and "wet appetites" for experiencing how God can transform us through our pain, which can be acted upon by entering a Level 2 small group.

We firmly believe that resurrecting hope is critical because it can literally mean the difference between life and death. You can go forty days without food, fifteen days without water and eight minutes without air, but you cannot go a second without hope. Hope is one of the essentials of life. In support of that, Dr. Harold Wolff of Cornell University conducted a study of 25,000 former POWs. In his study he discovered one group of POWs that showed minimal effect from all the physical and emotional torture they received. In this group were found the only ones who had a high level of hope.

Where do you go to find that hope? You go to the God of hope. Romans 15:13 says, *"May the God of hope fill you with all joy and peace as you trust in Him..."* So, in this program we will focus on the **Three Truths About Life** and how these truths can produce the encouragement necessary to admit to our needs and commit to making healthy changes in our life by accepting and beginning God's process of transformation. This program also focuses on showing our members that H.O.P.E. is a safe place where they are accepted and can find the hope, help and support needed to pursue a transformed life.

Goals

1. To resurrect hope.
2. To show that help can be found here and in Jesus Christ.
3. To show that this is a safe place to express our true feelings.
4. To expose the needs that we all have while dealing with the pain in our lives and point our members to the only real place where they can go to have those needs met.
5. To show our members that they are not alone and we will work through their pain with them.

6. To help our members begin to develop a safe and healthy support network.
7. To "wet appetites" for starting the process of transformation, while tearing down barriers to beginning this process.
8. To bring our members to the point where they are ready to get serious about making healthy changes in their life and commit to joining a *Names of H.O.P.E.* Level 2 group.

In essence, this book is about taking our members who come from a wide range of emotional and spiritual backgrounds and "funneling" them down to a more common place that includes:

1. A serious desire for transformation.
2. An openness to learn God's principles and truth.
3. A willingness to investigate God's plan for their pain and their future.

Regardless of what you are experiencing and how much pain you are in, we want to help you begin to feel hopeful that things can and will get better and that you do not have to continue living in pain forever. In fact, the goal of resurrecting hope can often have an immediate response. We have often witnessed how just attending our group for the first time and seeing that there are other hurting people present (as well as people who want to help them overcome their pain) can enable our members to immediately begin to experience the power of hope.

The format that we use to accomplish these goals is to follow the **Three Truths About Life** and the **Three Encouragements** that we can gain from these truths. In doing so, we gradually expose our members to truth that can be applied to their situation and pain. Since truth comes from the Word of God, we use the Bible as the source of truth and each lesson contains Scriptures to be memorized. This empowers our members for life by transforming the thoughts that dwell in their minds. In doing so, we replace the thoughts that are based on lies with thoughts that are based on the truth of God's Word.

Our approach to helping people overcome their pain and experience emotional health is based on the principle that emotional issues result from underlying spiritual needs. Emotional health and spiritual health are entwined; they cannot be separated. So we believe that by addressing spiritual needs you can successfully enable transformation that produces emotional wholeness and healing. In this way, we believe we are appropriately addressing the disease and not just the symptoms.

We realize that some of you may be hearing these things for the very first time. So to be perfectly clear, it does not matter where you are in your life right now as it pertains to learning about God and reading, studying, learning and memorizing the Bible. No matter where you are, it is OK. As our Guidelines say, we accept you as you are. All we want from you for right now is a desire and willingness to learn about God and the truth from His Word, and how it can apply to (and offer freedom from) your pain.

At this point, we are only asking for you to be open to giving our program an extended opportunity. We are going to take all of this one moment at a time, one day at a time and one step at a time, because there is simply no other way to go through it. Change takes time. You cannot rush it. You did not get to this painful point in your life overnight and you cannot escape from it overnight, either. It does not work that way.

But enough of the bad news, the good news is that we designed our ministry with these concepts in mind. Our multiple levels are designed to empower you for success throughout the entire process of transformation. (As previously mentioned, this *Doorway to H.O.P.E.* group is Level 1 of our three level ministry model). We will help you every level of the way, through the baby steps and the major milestones. So if you are open to investigating these things further, we are here to help you.

But we are not only here to help you learn and understand the truth, we are also here to support and encourage you throughout this entire process of transformation. We are here to walk with you through your pain and help you move away from your previous unhealthy community into a new one that is both healthy and Biblically based. Therefore, in addition to our groups, we also want to help you develop a support network that provides further strength and encouragement. Because this process is so important, it continues in and through all the levels of our transformation model.

So as you progress through our program, we will be helping you add to your support network. One particularly important addition to your network that is explained in Lesson 13 of the Level 2 book, *Names of H.O.P.E.*, is what we call a **Sp**iritual and **E**motional **C**oach, or a SPEC. A SPEC's contribution is to not only offer additional encouragement, understanding, instruction and guidance with the lessons you are learning, but also to help you apply them. They will be coaching you along the way in a one-on-one mentor type of a relationship.

There is a strategic reason why SPECs enter our program in Lesson 13 of Level 2, but there is no reason for you to wait until then for a SPEC to enter into ***your*** support network. It is never too early to begin utilizing the benefits of a SPEC. So if you are interested in pursuing a SPEC at any point in our program, let your leader know and they will help you get started by explaining the guidelines for finding a SPEC in Lesson 13 of *Names of H.O.P.E.*

Finally, if you need additional help, further explanation of things, someone else to talk with, or whatever else we may be able to provide, ask your leader. We will do all we can to help you experience and live out a transformed life.

The Lessons

The lessons are divided into five sections:

1. **Why Are You Here?**
2. **Truth**
3. **Checking In**
4. **Acting on the Truth**
5. **Transforming Benefits**

Why Are You Here? contains the background material for the topic being presented and contains *Leading Questions* at strategic locations to help generate discussion.

Truth boils the information presented in the lesson down to the life changing "take home message" of the truth.

Checking In is a time for each member to share what has been happening to them the previous week, how they feel about these events and provide feedback on the previous lesson's **Acting on the Truth** section. This builds accountability for our members as they work through the action items. The **Checking In** time is to be done according to the ***Doorway to H.O.P.E.*** **Guidelines** found in this lesson. At the end of each member's time, they are to say, "I'm in" signifying that their time is completed. If a member does not want to share, we still require them to at least say, "I'm in."

Acting on the Truth includes a practical plan of action to be taken during the week following the lesson. Efforts and progress on these steps are meant to be discussed at the next group meeting during **Checking In.**

Transforming Benefits explains the emotional rewards and hope generated as a result of completing the action steps.

Doorway to H.O.P.E. Guidelines

1. ***Safety.*** Our objective is to make our groups a place where we can feel safe to be vulnerable. Members will need to determine their own safety zones and what goes beyond those zones. The goal is to have everyone feel safe enough to expand those comfort zones as time elapses. If a discussion goes beyond a safety zone, the participant may excuse themselves from the group (just please let us know if you are only leaving for the week or for the remainder of the course).
2. ***Confidentiality.*** This is a necessity (except in a rare case where a person's safety and health is threatened and the responsible thing is to do otherwise. For example: threat of physical harm to self or others, child abuse or neglect, adult abuse, etc., plus issues that require consultation by the group leader with the other group leaders). We want everyone to feel free and safe to share his or her issues without the threat of ridicule, judgment or exposure.
    i. In the event of a breach of confidentiality, the responsible individual will be required to address the entire group and we will handle it in the group setting.
3. ***Acceptance.*** The basic principle that defines H.O.P.E. is that we are here to welcome anyone who comes to us for help. H.O.P.E. is not a social club, a private club or a clique. We are here to welcome everyone, along with their problems and pain.
    i. This means that we are very serious about not allowing any other agendas to develop within the ministry that conflict with our principles, goals, purpose, vision and guidelines. If you see or experience a problem in this area at any time that you are a member of one of our H.O.P.E. groups, please bring it to the attention of your group leader.
4. ***This is not therapy***. The leaders are not here for advice. As a transformation group, we are here to support, encourage and assist you on your journey through God's process of transformation. By sharing our stories we will gain strength as a group. But what is shared should not be interpreted as direct advice from the leaders of the group. If more intensive therapy is desired, we can refer you to individuals who can help you pursue that independently of this group.
5. ***Accountability.*** The participation and actions of all H.O.P.E. members are accountable to the other group members, leaders and the guidelines of H.O.P.E. H.O.P.E. is not a spectator sport and we will not enable those who seek our help to develop into spectators. Neither will we allow H.O.P.E. members to act in a manner that deviates from our purpose, principles or guidelines.
    i. For leadership accountability, we will not meet with group members of the opposite sex alone outside of the group. However, if needed, the leaders will make themselves available to group members by telephone, email or group meetings.

(In all situations, a third party is highly recommended in meetings, on conference calls or copied on written communications). Plus, we highly encourage group members to meet in safe situations outside of the group and develop their support networks.

6. ***First person focus.*** When issues directly involve other parties, we will limit our remarks to those in the first person. We will not allow the "bashing" of others. We are not here to criticize, condemn or attack others; we are here to support you. It is important that the focus remains on you and therefore discussions that deviate from that will not be tolerated. During the time of **Checking In**, we also ask that you limit your remarks to 3-5 minutes in order to give everyone equal opportunity to share.
7. ***The person speaking during Checking In has the floor.*** When someone is Checking In, other group members are not to interrupt them. **Checking In** is to be free from disruptions, interruptions, criticism or judgmental comments. As long as the information you share is focused on how you feel about it or how it is affecting you (good, bad or ugly), we want to hear about it. What you share can be directly related to a topic from the lessons, totally unrelated to the lesson topics and about something happening in your life right now, or somewhere in between.
    i. If a member's Checking In gets "off track" or becomes inappropriate, it is the group leader's responsibility to direct them back on course. At the completion of a member's Checking In, if other group members want to share supportive and encouraging remarks, that is OK. In fact, we encourage it. Just remember Guideline 4 and that this is not therapy and those comments are not to be interpreted as professional advice.
8. ***Prayer.*** We would appreciate members praying for the other group members. This will be beneficial in providing the support network necessary for courage and renewed strength to take action on the road to transformation.

Other Useful Information

<u>Leader's Note:</u> In addition to the other information presented in this section, we also recommend that you clearly state your local policy on charging for the books. We have always made some scholarships available for those who simply cannot afford to pay for a book. We further recommend handling these financial matters in a delicate manner to avoid embarrassment and allow all members to feel welcome. If your location can afford to do so, having scholarships for those who cannot pay will help eliminate yet another barrier that might keep someone from joining H.O.P.E.

To eliminate another barrier to people joining H.O.P.E., we also highly recommend providing free childcare for your groups. We have found that a significant number of single parents join our groups and by providing childcare it has made it much easier for them to attend. So if you are in a location that is equipped to provide childcare in a safe environment, this will eliminate one more barrier that might keep someone from joining H.O.P.E.

Finally, as the action steps are accomplished and the emotional rewards are gained, we highly recommend that these achievements be celebrated throughout this entire process. We believe times of celebration and fun are crucial parts of the journey through God's process of transformation. One way we like to celebrate in H.O.P.E. is the game show week that is built into the program in Lesson 10. Please take a look at the *Leader's Notes* in this lesson prior to that week so you can prepare something fun for your members. But in addition to the game show, we also recommend planning other social events when possible (like a BBQ, or bowling, or a movie night, etc.). We have experienced this to go a long way to making someone feel accepted and valued as a member of their group.

1. The **Acting on the Truth** section for this lesson is a little different than the others because we have two forms we highly suggest that our members fill out (which are found at the end of this lesson). The first is our **Contract for Membership in the *Doorway to H.O.P.E.* Group**. It states they are willing to give this program a try for the next 12 lessons. It is intended for self-accountability purposes only and should be kept just between themselves and God. Second, we recommend that each member fill out a **H.O.P.E. Group Member Contact Information Form**. This information is kept confidential. It is simply used to provide us with contact information for our members. This form can be copied and distributed to the group members (or your own version can be created).
2. Group leaders are facilitators, we are here as group members as well as leaders.
3. Childcare is provided at some of our locations, so if you are in need of this service, please ask your leaders if childcare will be provided at your location.
4. After this program has been completed, we will create new *Names of H.O.P.E.* Level 2 small groups for you to join. Level 2 is for those who are serious about pursing God's process of transformation, which we firmly hope will include you. Your experience in H.O.P.E. and with God's process of transformation is simply not complete unless you continue on with Level 2. At the end of this program, we will again use a **Contract for Membership in the *Names of H.O.P.E.* Group**.
5. Unless specifically noted otherwise, all Scripture references are taken from the New International Version (NIV) of the Bible. Other versions cited include the New American Standard Version (NASV) and the New Living Translation (NLT). In addition, all pronouns that refer to God have been capitalized out of reverence, regardless of the translation used.

Checking In

<u>*Leader's Note:*</u> Each week the lessons are presented in a "classroom" setting and everyone in Level 1 attends together. Following the completion of each lesson, the members of Level 1 then divide up into smaller groups (6-10 people, including a leader and co-leader, if available) for **Checking In**.

However, these smaller groups are ***not*** defined small groups. The whole point of Level 1 is to generate small groups for Level 2. So in this level we encourage our members to find a comfortable smaller group before finalizing and closing the Level 2 small groups. Plus, since new members can join this level any week, the Level 1 smaller groups used for **Checking In** have to remain dynamic to allow for the possibility of weekly changes.

Therefore, we highly recommend that you encourage your members to try different groups until they find a comfortable one (this applies to the smaller group leaders, too). Once they do, encourage them to stay with that group. Then you can utilize the smaller groups that are comfortable with one another to create your Level 2 small groups. These dynamics will allow you to create Level 2 small groups that have a much greater chance of being successful. We also recommend that you remind them weekly that the smaller groups in this level are not set yet, and that changes could occur from week to week.

Because of these dynamics, your location will need to develop a leadership team to successfully run this program. In addition to having leaders for each smaller group in Level 1, having multiple leaders in this level allows your location to rotate who presents the lesson each week. Because the need for multiple leaders continues through each level of our model, please consider this ahead of time and begin by developing your leadership team.

In dividing up into smaller groups each week, we first recommend that one of your leaders be the Smaller Groups Coordinator, preferably someone other than the person who generally presents the lessons (to prevent any of your leaders from being overwhelmed with responsibilities each week). When the lesson is completed, have your Smaller Groups Coordinator take over.

Your Smaller Groups Coordinator should begin by explaining the process and dynamics of dividing up into smaller groups, which can easily be completed by reading the information provided in this *Leader's Note*. Have them also explain that when issues arise related to the smaller groups, your members are to contact him or her. We also recommend that they read the Guidelines each week before dividing up into smaller groups. In particular, when it comes to the Confidentiality Guideline, we recommend that they apply it to the smaller groups. Therefore, whatever is shared in the smaller groups stays there and is not repeated to others in the Level 1 group as a whole.

When it comes to dividing up into smaller groups, you can imagine that sometimes specific topics and/or gender can be an issue. However, our experience has clearly shown that the material and groups can work very well among members of mixed genders or members who are struggling with completely different issues. In fact, we have had members of both genders request a mixed gender group because they wanted to be in a group that allowed for feedback from both genders. We have had very successful groups comprised of mixed genders, mixed topics of struggle, and even ones where the leader was a different gender than all the group members.

On the other hand, one could easily envision situations where these dynamics might not work well and could even be counterproductive. It simply depends on the individuals involved (which applies to both leaders and members).

Because we believe it is impossible to predetermine the dynamics that would work best in each situation, we have chosen ***not*** to develop or promote this ministry as one that requires the separation of genders or topics. Rather, we allow (and recommend) that each location determine the group dynamics that will work best in their situation. We believe this approach enables each location to have a greater impact and a greater chance of success by doing what is best for them.

But not only that, we have experienced what is commonly referred to as a "numbers game" when dividing up into smaller groups in Level 1 and creating small groups in Level 2. Sometimes a location can have its "hands tied" simply by the number of members who attend that are of one gender or that are struggling with a particular issue. If our ministry adopted a policy where we predetermined how small groups should "look", it could easily (and often) prevent us from ministering to a large number of people who came to us for help, which would defeat the purpose of our existence. As our Guidelines say, we accept all who come to us for help.

Therefore, when forming groups in your location, please use the appropriate amount of discretion and discernment. If your location requires, is better suited for, or has the "numbers" to allow for gender and/or topic specific groups, then utilize such groups.

If not, then do not. Our recommendation is simply to do whatever is appropriate for your location.

Finally, as we do with the lessons, it is also a good idea to begin and end **Checking In** with a time of prayer. You can begin with a general prayer and end with a more specific prayer that addresses the issues brought up during **Checking In**.

Please adhere to the ***Doorway to H.O.P.E.* Guidelines** while **Checking In.**

Please use this time today to talk about anything you are comfortable with sharing. At the completion of your time, we would like you to say, "I'm in" signifying that your time is completed. If you do not want to share this week, that is fine. But we still require you to at least say, "I'm in."

To help you get started, you may want to address the following statements and questions:

1. Briefly introduce yourself.
2. Why are you here and what expectations do you have from this group?
3. Have you been in a group like this before and what was it like?
4. How do you feel about being here?
5. What would you like the rest of us to know about you? Tell us something interesting about yourself. Maybe it is a hobby or where you have lived or what you do for a living, or what you like to do for fun, etc., but share something that will help us get to know you better.

Acting on the Truth

1. Read the **Contract for Membership in the *Doorway to H.O.P.E.* Group** on the page following this section. After reading it, make a decision on whether or not you want to commit to the contract by signing it and keeping it in a place where you will see it regularly.
2. If you commit to joining the group, please fill out the **H.O.P.E. Group Member Contact Information Form** on the final page of this lesson and turn it in to the *Doorway to H.O.P.E.* leader. To be clear, your information is not shared with anyone outside H.O.P.E. It is so we can contact you during the week if needed. You can simply make a copy of this form from the book.

Contract for Membership in the *Doorway to H.O.P.E.* Group

I, ________________________________, do hereby agree to become a member of the *Doorway to H.O.P.E.* Group. I will give God the time to complete the 12 lessons in the book and be open to hearing what He has to say to me about my pain and my situation in life. During this time I will commit to:

1. Attending all the group meetings.
2. Being an active participant in this program.
3. Honestly and diligently doing the homework in **Acting on the Truth**.
4. Being honest to myself and to God about my life and my pain.
5. Being open to making any changes God may want me to make.

This contract **is intended to be used as an agreement between you and God**. If you pledge to do this, please sign and date below and keep this contract in a place where you will see it regularly during the time it takes to complete the 12 lessons in the book.

Thank you for choosing to begin your journey through God's process of transformation. You will not regret it.

Signature: ____

Date: ____________________________

H.O.P.E. Group Member Contact Information Form

Name:____

Address: ____

City/state:_______________________________________

Phone:____________________ Work:____________________

Cell:_____________________ Email:____________________

H.O.P.E. Group Member Emergency Contact Information

Name:____

Relationship: _____________________________________

Address: ____

City/state:_______________________________________

Phone:____________________ Work:____________________

Cell:_____________________ Email:____________________

Voluntary Additional Information

Doctor:____

Counselor:_______________________________________

Conditions:______________________________________

Medications:_____________________________________

Other:____

____

Three Truths About Life

"Blessed are the poor in spirit, for theirs is the kingdom of heaven."
(Matthew 5:3)

However, this verse as it applies to our lessons, could be translated better as:

"Blessed are those who recognize their need for God."

Lesson 2

Why Are You Here?

"Then you will know the truth, and the truth will set you free."
(John 8:32)

Why Are You Here?

Leader's Note: Before beginning the lesson, we have found it helpful to use an icebreaker. Therefore, we have included a few trivia questions for you. We also like to have some prizes on hand (usually candy) for those who answer the trivia questions correctly.

Week 1: Trivia

1. On Happy Days, what was Fonzie's real name? (Arthur Fonzerelli)
2. Who lived at 704 Houser Street, Queens, NY? (The Bunkers)

3. On Green Acres, what was Arnold the pig's last name? (Ziffel)
4. Where did Herman Munster work? (At a funeral parlor)
5. What state has the highest percentage of people who walk to work? (Alaska)
6. What state is the Palmetto state? (South Carolina)
7. What state's motto is "Liberty and Independence?" (Delaware)
8. What was the original color of Coca-cola? (Green)
9. What is the average number of laughs a person has in one day? (17)
10. What is the most common street name in the US? (Park)

Leader's Note: After asking all the questions, share your gifts with anyone who may not have answered a question correctly. Then ask the following questions.

Leading Questions: Other than to get a fabulous prize by answering the trivia questions correctly, why are you here? What are your expectations for this group?

Leader's Note: After hearing the answers from group members, tell them why you personally are here.

As we have just heard, we all have our own reasons for being here. The reasons are many and cover a wide variety of issues. Think about the answers we just heard (and if you were not comfortable sharing your reason for being here, just think about yours in conjunction with everything else you just heard). These reasons for being here, the struggles in our lives, all point to three truths about life.

The Three Truths About Life:

1. We all live through painful experiences that can cause emotional wounds (some of which can be hidden).
2. Emotional wounds take longer to heal than physical wounds, but they can still be healed.
3. Jesus Christ wants to heal your emotional wounds.

From these three truths, we can also discover three encouragements.

The Three Encouragements from the Three Truths:

1. Regardless of the number or severity of your emotional wounds, you are ***not alone***. Even though it may feel like you are, there are others who have been through similar things that you have been through and feel the way you do. That is why all of us are here; we know how it feels to live through painful experiences.

2. Something ***can*** be done about your pain.
3. There is someone who actually ***wants*** to help and do something about it.

We all want to do something about our pain:

We all want to make it stop!

Not only do we want to make it stop, but we also want to make it stop now! You have undoubtedly come here in an effort to stop the pain. That may be your main focus right now.

However, most of us have never learned the truth about how to successfully deal with our pain. This unfortunately puts us in a dangerous position, one where we grasp at anything that offers us immediate relief. Sadly though, this will result in disastrous consequences. We end up developing coping mechanisms that actually prolong our pain and make it worse.

It becomes a vicious cycle where we end up feeling trapped. Our emotional health ends up being held hostage.

Fortunately, there is an answer. There is a better way, one that has been proven to be successful. This way is successful because it is not based on lies or faulty information; it is based on the truth. This way not only can give you back your life, but can also give you a better life.

This way is God's way and it follows His process for how to work through our pain. As Jesus said in John 14:6, "*I am the way and the truth and the life.*"

But there is a premise for this way to be successful. In order to embrace this way and follow God's process, you must first recognize you have a need. Even though your need to deal with your pain is legitimate (and we are committed to helping you with that), we would like to submit that you might have an even greater need. A need that you may not even be aware of yet.

Therefore, the purpose of this program is to help you recognize your needs.

If a person never realizes they are sick, they will never seek medical help for their illness. Living this way can only lead to tragedy. Jesus addressed this very point and explained His role in meeting our emotional and spiritual needs when he said in Matthew 9:12, "*It is not the healthy who need a doctor, but the sick.*"

For the remaining weeks in this program, we will expand upon the **Three Truths About Life** by presenting a topic that will help you discover your deeper needs. We will also expand upon the **Three Encouragements** by presenting the truths in such a way as to give you hope that your needs can be met by Jesus Christ.

Our process will be based on the truth, the Word of God. The truth of His Word contains the power you need to overcome the lies you have been taught and to overcome your pain. We read this truth in John 8:32 where Jesus said, "*Then you will know the truth, and the truth will set you free.*"

More truth we want to expand upon at this point relates to this ministry. We want you to know that in spite of how you may feel right now, the truth is that:

1. **You are not alone.** We will be here to help you and walk with you through whatever it is that brought you here in the first place. We are dedicated to seeing you overcome your pain and experience the fullness of life God has to offer you. We are passionate about this because we, too, have been there and know how it feels.
2. **You are accepted.** The basic principle that we operate under is that we are here to welcome anyone who comes to us for help. H.O.P.E. is not a social club, a private club or a clique. We are here to welcome all who come to us, along with their problems and pain.
   i. What this means is that we are very serious about not allowing any other agendas to develop within the ministry that conflict with our principles, mission and vision.
   ii. If you experience a problem in this area (or any other area) at any time that you are a member of one of our H.O.P.E. groups, please bring it to the attention of your group leader. We will do all we can to ensure everyone's safety and acceptance.
3. **You are loved.** Again, not only does God love you, but we do, too. We are here to pass along to you the same love we have received from God and from others who have helped us. Love is a powerful medicine, as we hope you will personally experience here from us.
4. **It is OK to talk about how you feel.** No matter how you are feeling, you cannot address it or make any changes about it unless you get it out in the open. You cannot heal a wound by saying it is not there. That is why our time for **Checking In** is so important. We hope that as time goes on, you will find that this really is a safe place to talk about how you feel, and that includes all of the good, the bad and the ugly.
5. **Healing your wounds will open the door to living the fullness of life God intended for you to live.** God never intended for you to live your life defeated by your emotional wounds and pain. He intended for you to overcome them and reap the rewards He

has for you. He wants you to experience a life of peace, joy and happiness. Not only that, He also provides the way to make that happen. You only have to choose whether or not you want to follow His way. We cannot encourage you strongly enough to make the right choice in this matter.

6. **The principles we follow to overcome pain and transform lives are based on reliance on Jesus Christ.** H.O.P.E. is about spreading the power of Jesus Christ to overcome and transform. He alone provides all we need to live a life of victory and fullness, so our objective is to always point you to Him as you journey towards emotional and spiritual wholeness and healing.
    i. The first step towards receiving the power of Jesus Christ in your life is to begin a personal relationship with Him. If you are unsure about doing this or even what it means, we will revisit this topic and further explain it during this program and the Level 2 *Names of H.O.P.E.* program. But you are also welcome to come and talk to one of our leaders at any time and we will be happy to discuss it more thoroughly with you.
7. **We will help you develop a support network.** One of the ways Jesus Christ provides for your needs as you journey toward emotional and spiritual wholeness and healing is through the development of a support network consisting of safe and healthy people. Being a member of H.O.P.E. is one part of that support network, but we will also help you expand your network beyond our weekly group meetings. This will continue and become more specific in the Level 2 *Names of H.O.P.E.* program.
    i. As you get comfortable with others in this program, we highly encourage you to exchange contact information so you can develop a relationship with people you can talk to during the week who know what you are experiencing. Please feel free to ask for contact information from the leaders so you can talk to one of them during the week, too.

As we complete the remaining lessons of this program, we will explore each of the truths we just mentioned much more thoroughly. As we do so, we will help you see why the right way to handle your emotional wounds and pain is God's way, the way of truth. We will continue to display the truth to you, while at the same time exposing the lies in your life so you will be able to clearly recognize them.

For now, we hope you will commit yourself to giving God a chance and patiently giving Him the time to show you what He can do in your life. Those of us in H.O.P.E. who have experienced God's transforming power can honestly tell you that you will not regret it.

Truth

The first step toward emotional wholeness and healing is to recognize that you have needs. Not only that, but to recognize that God wants to meet your needs. He wants to do this because He loves us unconditionally. Nehemiah 9:32 describes God as, "*...our God, the great, mighty and awesome God, who keeps His covenant of love...*" We have God's Word on it, and you will never find a better guarantee than that. God's love for us is a truth we will discuss further in Lesson 5.

The underlying concept for overcoming emotional wounds and pain involves transforming your mind with the truth. It is a process where you replace wrong thinking (based on the lies you have been taught) with right thinking (based on God's Truth). As it says in Romans 12:2, "*And do not be conformed to this world, but be transformed by the renewing of your mind, that you may prove what the will of God is, that which is good and acceptable and perfect*" (NASV).

If you are feeling trapped in your pain today, take heart because there is a way that you can be set free. It is a way that has not only been proven successful to many of us in this ministry, but also a way that can be successful for you.

> Leader's Note: Before dividing up into smaller groups, go through the ***Doorway to H.O.P.E.* Guidelines** found in Lesson 1 on page 22. Each following week, have the smaller group leaders review them prior to beginning **Checking In** and remind them to pray before and after each time of **Checking In**.

Checking In

Let's take a minute to review the **Guidelines for Checking In** found in Lesson 1.

Please use this time today to talk about anything you are comfortable with sharing. You can share what has been happening lately in your life or how you feel about what we just discussed. Regardless of the issue, focus on how you feel about it and how it is affecting you.

At the completion of your time, we would like you to say, "I'm in" signifying that your time is completed. If you do not want to share this week, that is fine. But we still require you to at least say, "I'm in."

To help you get started, you may want to address the following statements and questions:

1. Briefly introduce yourself.
2. Why are you here and what expectations do you have from this ministry?
3. Have you been in a group like this before and what was it like?
4. How do you feel about being here?

Acting on the Truth

1. Why are you here? What brought you here?

 ____

 ____

 ____

 ____

2. Spend time this week focusing on the fact that God really wants to meet your needs. Repeat this to yourself throughout the week.
3. Begin transforming your mind with God's truth by memorizing John 8:32, "*Then you will know the truth, and the truth will set you free.*" Each time you say it, spend time thinking about what it means for you and your situation.
4. Continue transforming your mind with God's truth by memorizing Nehemiah 9:32, "*...our God, the great, mighty and awesome God, who keeps His covenant of love...*" Each time you say it, spend time thinking about what it means for you and your situation.
5. Continue transforming your mind with God's truth by memorizing Romans 12:2, "*And do not be conformed to this world, but be transformed by the renewing of your mind, that you may prove what the will of God is, that which is good and acceptable and perfect*" (NASV). Each time you say it, spend time thinking about what it means for you and your situation.

Transforming Benefits

1. **Begin replacing wrong thinking with right thinking.** By focusing on the truth of God, you can begin to change your pattern of thinking from wrong thinking to right thinking. This is a very healthy change. You can begin to replace the lies that have been the base of your belief system with the truth. A great way to begin doing that is by repeating to yourself that you ***do*** matter to God and He loves you.
2. **Begin transforming your mind by dwelling on God's truth.** By memorizing the scripture verses, you will begin filling your mind and heart with God's Truth. You are what you think. Proverbs 23:7 says, "*For as he thinks within himself, so he is*" (NASV). What we think about and dwell on will affect our feelings, which in turn affects our attitudes, which ultimately, affects our behavior. You can begin to transform all of these by spending increasing amounts of time thinking about truth. The most important thing you can think about in life is God.
3. **Accountability to yourself and God.** By signing our contract, you become accountable to yourself and to God for honestly trying something new and completing this program, while being open to any changes God wants you to make.

Truth 1: We All Experience Emotional Pain

"In this world you will have trouble. But take heart!
I have overcome the world."
(John 16:33)

Lesson 3

You Are Not Alone

"The LORD Himself goes before you and will be with you; He will never leave you nor forsake you. Do not be afraid; do not be discouraged."
(Deuteronomy 31:8)

Why Are You Here?

<u>*Leading Question:*</u> Have any of you signed your contract? To be clear, you do ***not*** have to share your answer one way or the other. But if any of you would like to tell us, we just want to applaud you. So if you are comfortable telling us, "How many of you signed your contract?" Give them a round of applause! We firmly believe you will not be disappointed.

Last week we discussed the <u>**Three Truths About Life**</u>:

1. We all live through painful experiences that can cause emotional wounds (some of which can be hidden).

2. Emotional wounds take longer to heal than physical wounds, but they can still be healed.
3. Jesus Christ wants to heal your emotional wounds.

For the next 4 Lessons, we will look at Truth Number 1 more closely and elaborate on the encouragement that we can find in this truth. As we said last week:

Regardless of the number or severity of your emotional wounds, you are not alone.

Looking at Truth Number 1 we find that we all live through painful experiences that can cause emotional wounds. The truth of the matter is that life hurts. It is an inescapable fact that at sometime we will all experience something that is emotionally painful.

In support of this, we have no doubt that your own painful stories and experiences have already come to mind as you are reading this. The pain may have been decades ago, years ago, months ago, days ago or all of the above (or it may come tomorrow), but we all know from experience just how painful life can be.

But there is also some good news that can be found in this truth. This truth can actually be very freeing once you realize that you are ***not*** a freak or an outcast because of your wounds and pain. Since we all live through pain, it stands to reason that this is arguably the one aspect of life where we all have the most in common. When it comes to the pain of life, we are all in the same boat!

Therefore, it is important to understand that we ***do not*** have to allow our pain to drag us through the mire of isolation, alienation and damaging behaviors. Rather, as we will show throughout all levels of this program:

Our pain can be utilized as an opportunity for extraordinary emotional and spiritual growth.

The key to reaping the positive benefits of your pain is to draw upon the experiences, encouragement, support, strength and direction of others who have "been there." Have you ever heard the expression, "There's safety in numbers?" Well, this notion is not only true when traveling through hostile territory; it is also true when it pertains to wrestling with our emotional pain. It is the reason why we are here. It is the reason why this ministry was started.

Leader's Note: What follows is my testimony, but this section is meant to be personalized with your testimony and why you are here. During the smaller groups, it will be very helpful to have your other leaders share their testimonies and why they are here, too. All of this will contribute to letting the new members know they are not alone.

There is no better way to encourage someone to keep going than through the sharing of personal testimonies, and the more testimonies they hear, the better. Our members need to hear that others have been there and made it through alive! They need to hear that other people just like them have gone through similar problems and that through the help of the Lord and caring people, things really can change and get better.

So use your own testimony here, or those you read about in books, newspapers, magazines, on the internet, or utilize guest speakers, etc., and provide handouts if you can. And do not stop this practice in this lesson; keep doing this throughout the entire program as opportunities arise.

Let me take a little time to give you some history on how H.O.P.E. began by sharing some of my experiences with you.

I have always struggled with two things, anger and depression. I come from a long line of volatile, competitive Grimms. When faced with a painful situation, my immediate response is to get angry about it. That is usually followed by my second response, to get depressed about it.

Growing up, I suffered from a lack of affirmation and acceptance. So I did everything I could to gain approval in these two areas. This resulted in my becoming a perfectionist. Anyone else who is a perfectionist knows that this lifestyle only lends itself to more failure and frustration, both of which fueled my anger and depression.

The 1980s was a particularly difficult decade for my battle with anger and depression. In 1981, after my girlfriend broke up with me, I attempted suicide. Another incident that kept my depression strong was my mother passing away from cancer in 1987.

During this time in my life, I cannot begin to tell you how many things I broke during fits of rage or how many drinks I had or how many drugs I did. On top of all the damage to myself, I also succeeded in damaging many relationships.

In spite of all this, I managed to get married in 1988 and get accepted into graduate school the same year at the University of Missouri. My marriage was rocky to say the least, and the many unhealthy decisions I made only contributed to the problems. With my emotional instabilities, it was often no picnic to live with me.

On September 15, 1991, during a time when my first wife and I were separated, I was back in my hometown for the weekend and went to my brother's church. On that Sunday morning, I heard the Gospel message and immediately knew that I needed Jesus in my life. I went forward that day and gave my life to Jesus Christ.

I would love to tell you that my life turned around immediately, but it did not. I still struggled, and so did my marriage. Yet I was able to achieve my Ph.D. in Molecular Biology in 1993 and I accepted a postdoctoral position that resulted in us moving to Maryland.

In 1996 I experienced a series of painful events that started with my first wife leaving me, followed soon after by my breaking my right hand. Immediately thereafter the engine in my truck died and I lost my transportation. Then I lost my position on the leadership team of the evangelism ministry at my church. Finally, I lost my church and a number of my friends there.

To make matters worse, my finances were a disaster as a result of my divorce. To give you an example of where I was financially, for the next 1-½ years I was making $400/month less than the sum total of my bills. That was before going to the grocery store or any other place. Then, the final painful event was when my dog Schatzie became a paraplegic after an accident that broke her back.

All these events happened in less than four months.

As you can imagine, I was not a "happy camper" and struggled mightily with my anger and depression. I again made a lot of unhealthy choices during this time. I have never felt so lonely and alone in my entire life. I was just sick of everything after my dog was hurt and I wanted to give up. I can still vividly picture the inside of her cage at the vet where I would climb inside, hold her, and cry.

But in spite of how much I wanted to give up, God refused to give up on me. He led me to a new church where I met my late friend and mentor Bob Poskitt. Shortly after meeting Bob, I started to attend his support group for men who were struggling with divorce. The first time I attended a meeting was one of the hardest things I have ever done in my life. Everything inside me screamed not to.

> Leading Question: How many of you felt that way about coming here? I want to applaud you for taking this step because I know how hard it can be.

But as he started to replace the lies in my mind with the truth, things inside me began to change. It definitely did not happen overnight, but things were changing slowly and steadily. I started to see my situation in a different light, the light of God's truth.

Not only that, but I began to see that there was actually a reason why all this pain came into my life. God had a plan for it all. As strange as that may sound, it is true. The plan had to do with me not getting angry about my pain or getting depressed about it, but learning how to embrace it and handle it in a positive, truthful and healthy way.

His plan began to unfold over the next several years, which included my meeting and marrying my wife Tiffany. We moved to the Chicago area in 2001 and not long afterwards starting attending a local church. A series of events led me to start thinking about God's plan for me, which was highlighted on January 6, 2002.

During his message on that Sunday, our pastor dared us to do something with our year for the Lord. I went up to him after that service and asked him how to start a new ministry. I did not even know yet what it would be, I only knew God wanted me to do something different than what was currently available.

Shortly after that, I can clearly remember sitting in our kitchen one evening and saying to my wife, "Maybe God's trying to tell me to start some kind of a support group." My wife replied, "I've known all along that's what God was preparing you to do and you'd be perfect for that." (This just goes to show how my wife lets me ***think*** I am the smart one!)

So H.O.P.E. was started in 2002, and as they say, the rest is history. As I started telling you at the beginning of this lesson, the reason this ministry was started was to help other people who were experiencing painful times like I did. Through my own life, I knew how it felt to hurt and God wanted to use that to draw more people to come and experience His healing power, to come and experience His hope.

I felt like God was telling me when I started this that I may be alone in this now, but others will come. They will come.

If you are hearing about God's hope and healing power for the first time, let me make clear that these aspects of Almighty God are definitely there and available to all, ***including you***, no matter how you feel right now or how bad your situation may be.

I told you a lot about the pain I experienced, but let me tell you about some of the ways God showed how much He cared about me and how real He is in my life.

In addition to my marriage to Tiffany, God provided the money I needed to pay my bills each month through various means. I never missed a payment and I never missed a meal. Out of that experience, one of my favorite verses has now become Psalm 37:25, "*I was young and now I am old, yet I have never seen the righteous forsaken or their children begging bread.*"

God provided a wheel cart for my dog Schatzie and the money to pay for it. I am glad to say she lived seven more happy years with her paralysis. He provided transportation through two neighbors during the months that I was without my truck. He provided a new church and new friends who were committed to helping me work toward emotional wholeness and healing.

God provided hedge trimmers. The day after mine broke I was driving to work complaining about my situation and how I could not even afford to buy new hedge trimmers. I literally had my head hanging out the window as I was driving so the roof of my vehicle would not interfere with God's reception. As I was yelling my complaints to God, I had to slow down because there was something in the road up ahead (even though my head was hanging out the window, I was still paying attention to the road!).

That something in the road turned out to be hedge trimmers. After waiting awhile, I picked them up and said, "Thank you" and had to ask forgiveness for doubting and complaining. Plus, they were much nicer than the ones I had previously owned!

God even provided me a book of stamps one day when I could not afford to buy them. I went to the post office to mail bills but realized I did not have enough money left over to buy stamps. I walked out of the post office feeling very dejected until I discovered a book of stamps lying on the ground next to my car.

<u>Leader's Note:</u> This is where my testimony ends.

So let's finish the same way we started:

You are not alone.

It is not just me, but this ministry is now full of people who know how you feel. Look at the others in your group and you will see what we mean. Others have indeed come. People who are here for the same reason H.O.P.E. was started, because they have lived through pain themselves and now want to help other people overcome their pain. People who want to help because they care and they want you to experience how much God cares, too.

People who understand what Paul meant when he wrote in 2 Corinthians 1:3-4, *"Blessed be the God and Father of our Lord Jesus Christ, the Father of mercies and God of all comfort; who comforts us in all our afflictions so that we may be able to comfort those who are in any affliction with the comfort with which we ourselves are comforted by God"* (NASV).

In 300 B.C., Plato said, "What a culture honors, it cultivates." At H.O.P.E., we honor the principle we just read in 2 Corinthians 1:3-4 to the glory of our Lord Jesus Christ. Because we honor this principle, we cultivate emotional and spiritual wholeness and healing.

Truth

You are not alone. In this world, you only have to travel next door to find others who are hurting. The world is full of hurting people because life hurts. Let's take a look at just a few examples (all statistics at the time of this publication):

- The current divorce rate is over 50%
- 40% of Americans will develop cancer at some point (1/2.2 men and 1/2.5 women)
- 1.5 million Americans suffer heart attacks annually
- 14 million Americans abuse alcohol
- Over half as many abuse illicit drugs
- 27% of high school girls report being victims of sexual or physical abuse
- 35 million Americans suffer from depression (16% of our population)
- The suicide rate jumped 200% over the last decade
- 20 million Americans suffer from anxiety

Convinced? Despite these statistics, we can take comfort in the fact that there is hope and there is help. Life may hurt, but God can heal. In John 16:33 Jesus said, *"In this world you will have trouble. But take heart! I have overcome the world."* Not only that, we have His Word that He will stick by us through our pain as we read in Proverbs 18:24, *"...there is a friend who sticks closer than a brother."*

If it were not enough that Jesus will stick with you in your pain, those of us in this ministry are also committed to doing that because we are passionate about helping people like you who are hurting. We, too, will be on your side and we will stand with you. We will help you overcome your pain just like someone did with us. We, too, will not leave you to go it alone. There is indeed safety in numbers.

Have you ever seen geese flying overhead in their typical V shaped formation? They fly like this because it is a very aerodynamic formation. All the geese draft off the point goose and thereby reduce wind resistance and make it much easier for them to fly. In fact, a biologist who studied this method of flight reported that geese can fly 71% farther in this formation than they could on their own.

But the point goose in this formation has to fly into the full brunt of the wind. It is much more difficult for that goose to fly because it feels the brunt of the wind resistance.

While watching them fly, have you ever listened to them? They are ***always*** honking while they fly in their V formation, all of them except the point goose.

Leading Question: Do you know why all the rest of the geese honk while they fly?

They honk as a way of encouraging the point goose to keep going and not give up. They all know how hard it is to fly in that position because they all take turns flying there.

Here is the point. When you know what it feels like to face the brunt of the wind, you are uniquely qualified to speak about your experience and spread encouragement.

Have you heard it said, "You are what you eat?" Well, it is also true that, "You are what you think." Proverbs 23:7 says, "*For as he thinks within himself, so he is*" (NASV).

If you have been thinking that you are alone, take courage in what we shared with you in this lesson because the truth is that you are not alone. This ministry is full of people who have faced the full brunt of the wind and overcame it and are now more than willing to encourage you to keep going and do the same.

Checking In

Take a minute to review the **Guidelines for Checking In** found in Lesson 1.

Please use this time today to talk about anything you are comfortable with sharing. You can share what has been happening lately in your life or how you feel about what we just discussed. Regardless of the issue, focus on how you feel about it and how it is affecting you.

At the completion of your time, we would like you to say, "I'm in" signifying that your time is completed. If you do not want to share this week, that is fine. But we still require you to at least say, "I'm in."

To help you get started, you may want to address the following statements and questions:

1. Briefly introduce yourself.
2. Why are you here and what expectations do you have from this ministry?
3. Have you been in a group like this before and what was it like?
4. How do you feel about being here?

Acting on the Truth

1. Do you feel alone or lonely? If so, describe how you feel.

 ____

 ____

 ____

 ____

2. Are you beginning to see that you are not alone?

 ____

 ____

 ____

 ____

3. Spend time this week focusing on the truth shared today that you are not alone. Repeat this to yourself often during the week.
4. Continue transforming your mind with God's truth by memorizing John 16:33, "*In this world you will have trouble. But take heart! I have overcome the world.*" Each time you say it, spend time thinking about what it means for you and your situation.
5. Continue transforming your mind with God's truth by memorizing Deuteronomy 31:8, "*The LORD Himself goes before you and will be with you; He will never leave you nor forsake you. Do not be afraid; do not be discouraged.*" Each time you say it, spend time thinking about what it means for you and your situation.

Transforming Benefits

1. **There is safety in numbers.** You can gain the encouragement, strength and courage you need to make positive, healthy changes in your life when you realize you are not alone and do not have to go through your pain alone.
2. **Continue transforming your mind by dwelling on God's truth.** By memorizing the scripture verses, you will begin filling your mind and heart with God's Truth. You are what you think. Proverbs 23:7 says, "*For as he thinks within himself, so he is*" (NASV). What we think about and dwell on will affect our feelings, which in turn affects our attitudes, which ultimately, affects our behavior. You can begin to transform all of these by spending increasing amounts of time thinking about truth. By memorizing and focusing on the truth in the verses that prove you are not alone, you can change how you think about your life and your status in relation to your painful situation.
3. **Overcoming fear of the future.** By accepting the truth that you will not have to go through your journey of transformation all by yourself, you can begin to overcome the fear you may have about being abandoned somewhere down the road in this process.

Truth 1: We All Experience Emotional Pain

"In this world you will have trouble. But take heart!
I have overcome the world."
(John 16:33)

Lesson 4

You Are Accepted

"Accept one another, then, just as Christ accepted you,
in order to bring praise to God"
(Romans 15:7)

Why Are You Here?

In Lesson 2 we discussed the **Three Truths About Life:**

1. We all live through painful experiences that can cause emotional wounds (some of which can be hidden).
2. Emotional wounds take longer to heal than physical wounds, but they can still be healed.
3. Jesus Christ wants to heal your emotional wounds.

Last week we looked at Truth Number 1 more closely and elaborated on the encouragement that we can find in this truth. As we said:

Regardless of the number or severity of your emotional wounds, you are not alone.

This week we will discuss more encouraging news from this truth.

Knowing that you are not alone is encouraging, but not enough. You can understand there are others who know how you feel, but if you cannot relate to them, it will not help.

You need to know that the others who feel your hurts will accept you as you are, in your pain and brokenness. You already have the qualifications for membership in this club that includes the entire human race, but you need to know your membership is accepted.

The second encouragement we want to share from Truth 1 is that:

You are accepted here with us!

The reason is that we know how you feel. We know how it feels to be broken and to be in pain. As we said last week, life hurts.

The irony in this truth is that it is actually ***normal*** to feel pain. But what is abnormal is the way many of us choose to deal with those feelings.

> *Leading Question:* How many of you came in here feeling normal because of your pain and hurts? (Remind them that their pain is normal but the unhealthy ways they try to deal with it is abnormal.)

Understanding that we know how it feels to live through hurt and pain is the key to understanding your acceptance. Once you know you are one of us and we are all in the same boat, it becomes easier to acknowledge and grab a hold of your acceptance.

We believe this is one of the main reasons why this ministry is successful in transforming lives. We know how it feels. The ability to empathize and speak from experience means that we have earned the right to be heard. It tears down barriers that in other circles would take years or decades to topple.

Let us illustrate this. There are five levels of small groups that have been described:

1. **Cliché** – superficial, patented, non-personal and rehearsed responses.
2. **Ideas and Facts** – sharing of personal statistics and information.
3. **Ideas and Opinions** – more honest and personal sharing that includes ideas and opinions.
4. **Feelings** – honest sharing of feelings.
5. **Peak** – honest sharing of insights, members are teachable, they invite input and they receive feedback well, there is full trust of others and things are done and said with the appropriate attitude and motives within a loving, truthful and honest community.

In a typical small group setting, it takes 9-18 months to attain the level of **Feelings** and 18-24 months to achieve the level of **Peak.** But we have consistently experienced that our H.O.P.E. small groups can start at the **Feelings** level and arrive at the **Peak** level in only a few weeks.

Since we have been there, too, and know how it feels, we can create an environment in H.O.P.E. where our members really do feel safe, accepted and are willing to talk about what they are experiencing.

Contrast the foundation of our ministry to a recent situation where the opposite was true.

On February 20, 2003, there was a deadly fire at a nightclub in West Warwick, Rhode Island, where almost 100 people died. A few days after the fire, one of the survivors of the fire was interviewed on a popular morning TV show by one of their news anchors. During the interview, the young man being interviewed said he was having problems dealing with "survivor's guilt", to which the news anchor replied, "I know how you feel."

When I heard the news anchor say that, I almost came unglued. There is no way on God's green earth that the news anchor knew how this young man felt unless they had been there. The look on the young man's face said it all; that was not what he wanted to hear.

In 1996, I experienced something very similar. I lived the entire 12 months of that year separated from my first wife leading up to our divorce. During that year, there were many people who came up to me with "advice." People who said, "You need to do this" or "You need to do that" or "You need to stop doing this or that." Quite often it also included a verse from the Bible explaining why they were giving me this advice.

But as this continued, I started to notice that many of these people who were offering me advice had never been through a divorce. I believe their intentions were good, but frankly,

I did not want to listen to anyone who did not have clue what I was experiencing or could not relate to how I felt.

This points to a valuable lesson:

It is often more important to listen than it is to speak.

Job experienced this, too. Job experienced the loss of his children, wealth and health. In the second chapter of Job, three of Job's friends visit him during his time of great pain. Job 2:13 says, "*Then they sat on the ground with him for seven days and seven nights. No one said a word to him, because they saw how great his suffering was.*"

The truth is, Job's three friends should have continued on in their silence. But they spent the next 35 chapters supposedly telling Job "how things really are." But God clearly explains the futility of everything they said when He answers in Job 38:2 with, "*Who is this that darkens My counsel with words without knowledge?*"

Ironically, too, in my situation, I do not remember a single bit of advice that was offered to me back in 1996 by those who had never been through a divorce. However, the one thing I do remember, as clearly as if it were yesterday, was when a man named Jim put his arm around me and said, "David, I don't have a clue what you're going through. But if you need anything, you just let me know."

Those of us in H.O.P.E. intimately know that you do not want to talk or listen to someone who does not have a clue what it is like to go through what you are going through, either. That is why we are here for you and we can say we accept you as you are in the midst of your hurt and pain. We do this because we know how it feels to be in your shoes.

Not only do we know how it feels, God does too. In the Garden of Gethsemane before He was unjustly arrested, we read this about Jesus in Matthew 26:38 where He said, "*My soul is overwhelmed with sorrow to the point of death. Stay here and keep watch with Me.*"

He knows, and because He knows, Jesus also knows how much we need to feel accepted. In fact, He has called us to accept one another. We read this in Romans 15:7 where it says, "*Accept one another, then, just as Christ accepted you, in order to bring praise to God.*"

Notice in this verse that it says, "*...just as Christ accepted you...*" So if it was not enough that we accept you with your hurt and pain, this verse also says that ***God accepts you, too!***

However, there is a premise to God's acceptance of us that needs to be addressed at this point. The Bible teaches that God accepts us based on His Son Jesus Christ. Through His death on the cross, Jesus became the one and only Savior for all of mankind. He became the way for us to be saved from the penalty of our sins and to have a relationship with Him (in this life and for all of eternity). That is why Jesus told us in John 14:6, *"I am the way and the truth and the life. No one comes to the Father except through Me."* In John 3:16 the Bible also says, *"For God so loved the world, that He gave His one and only Son, that whoever believes in Him shall not perish but have eternal life."*

Therefore, God ultimately accepts those into eternity who have accepted His Son Jesus Christ as their Savior. Because of its paramount importance, we will discuss this further throughout this book (particularly in the next lesson and in Lesson 12) and in the Level 2 book *Names of H.O.P.E.*

But whether or not you have made this decision, your pain and wounds do ***not*** mean that God is against you. Romans 8:31 says, *"If God is for us, who can be against us?"* Think about that for a moment. If God Himself is on our side, then who or what can be against us?

If you have not yet accepted Jesus Christ as your Savior, your wounds and pain do ***not*** mean that God will not accept you. On the contrary, He is waiting to accept you with His arms open wide. He wants you to come to Him now so you can spend eternity with Him. In fact, God may very well be using your pain to open your eyes to what He offers you through the acceptance of His Son. In 2 Peter 3:9 we read, *"The Lord is not slow in keeping His promise, as some understand slowness. He is patient with you, not wanting anyone to perish, but everyone to come to repentance."*

If you have already accepted Jesus Christ as your Savior, your wounds and pain are also ***not*** indicators that God has turned His back on you or abandoned you. (It should be pointed out here that there are times when our painful circumstances result from sin in our lives. When this is the case, the sin needs to be repented of and turned away from.) God often allows pain in our lives as a tool to mold us into His image, to show us how much we need Him and to build our faith (by showing us how much He can be trusted). (These concepts will be discussed in great detail in the Level 2 book *Names of H.O.P.E.*)

So regardless of your need, whether it is for salvation, strength, forgiveness, healing, deliverance, transformation, faith, your daily bread, etc., you can go to the Lord just as you are and He will accept you and your plea. God will accept you as you are, in your current condition, if you decide to come to Him and accept what He offers through His Son Jesus Christ.

Not only do you need to come to God, you need to ***run to Him*** and what He offers. The ironic thing is that we humans have a bad habit of running ***from*** God when things go bad. We blame God; we get mad at Him and we move away from Him because we think the painful circumstances in our life are evidence that God is not on our side (which the devil just loves because we are playing right into his nefarious hands).

But we need to reverse that trend and move ***toward*** God because He is the ***only true*** source of all the help we need. Our circumstances have no bearing whatsoever on God's acceptance of us. In most cases God will actually use your painful experiences to get your attention so you will recognize how much you need Him. God will go to great lengths, including the use of pain, to draw you to Him and what He offers.

Please grab hold of the truth that God accepts you. Stop believing the lie that God is against you so you will be free to run to Him. Once you do, you open yourself up to stop living a defeated life and start living the victorious, fulfilled life that Jesus intended and designed you to live.

Understanding your acceptance by God and this ministry is critical because the need to feel accepted is part of one of the basic needs that we all have, the need to feel secure. The need to feel secure and the need to feel significant make up the two key elements of the most basic need in all of us, the need to feel worthwhile. (This is a principle that has been outlined in several of the books written by Dr. Larry Crabb, e.g. *Basic Principles of Biblical Counseling*).

Because of its direct correlation with emotional and spiritual health, we will expand upon this principle in this book and in the Level 2 book *Names of H.O.P.E.* Starting with the next lesson, we will continue with this concept by discussing how in addition to acceptance, God can also provide the other main ingredient in our need to feel secure, love.

Truth

Feeling accepted is a huge part of feeling secure, and we want you to know that you are accepted here. Maybe you came here feeling just the opposite because of your life history and experiences, but the truth is that you are accepted here. We have been called to accept you in Romans 15:7 where it says, *"Accept one another, then, just as Christ accepted you, in order to bring praise to God."*

As we read in this verse, not only are you accepted here, but God accepts you as well. His acceptance of all of us is ultimately based on our acceptance of His Son Jesus Christ as our Savior. It is ***not*** based on our painful experiences in life.

As part of accepting you, we will be here to listen to you, share our experiences with you and encourage you. We will cry with you, sit and be quiet with you, shout with you, or whatever else you need. Being accepted means this is a safe place for you to express your true emotions without the fear of ridicule, chastisement or rejection.

The basic principle that we operate under is:

We are here to welcome anyone who comes to us for help.

H.O.P.E. is not a private club or a clique. We are here to welcome all who come to us, along with their problems and pain. And that includes you.

We can do this because we, too, have been there and earned our stripes, so to speak. God has brought us through the storms in our lives in order that we can be in the unique position to be able to both sympathize and empathize with you. We have earned that right by living the life we have lived. We accept you and are committed to seeing you through your situation and bringing you to a place where you can overcome it and experience wholeness and healing.

Your pain is normal. As we are learning in Truth 1, we all have at least one wound or emotional scar. How many of us choose to deal with our pain is what is abnormal. Not only is it abnormal, it is also extremely dangerous. The list of unhealthy behaviors we adopt to deal with our pain is very long. The irony is that a primary reason we act this way is to gain acceptance and security, but these unhealthy methods will never meet this need.

Ultimately, it is only a personal God that can meet the need for acceptance and security for personal beings. In John 10:28,29 Jesus said, "*...no one can snatch them out of My hand. My Father, who has given them to Me, is greater than all; no one can snatch them out of My Father's hand.*" God can be trusted to provide the security we all crave. We have His Word on it.

Checking In

Take a minute to review the **Guidelines for Checking In** found in Lesson 1.

Please use this time today to talk about anything you are comfortable with sharing. You can share what has been happening lately in your life or how you feel about what we just discussed. Regardless of the issue, focus on how you feel about it and how it is affecting you.

A good way to get started is by telling the people in your group about how you handled and answered the items from last week's **Acting on the Truth** section. Or maybe you might want to tell them if any of the items were particularly difficult to deal with or hard to understand. You may also tell them if any of the things we just discussed are difficult for you to understand or accept.

At the completion of your time, we would like you to say, "I'm in" signifying that your time is completed. If you do not want to share this week, that is fine. But we still require you to at least say, "I'm in."

To help you get started, you may want to address the following statements and questions:

1. Briefly introduce yourself.
2. Why are you here and what expectations do you have from this ministry?
3. Have you been in a group like this before and what was it like?
4. How do you feel about being here?

Acting on the Truth

1. How have you pursued acceptance and security from other people?

____

____

____

____

2. Do you realize yet that you are accepted by God and by H.O.P.E.?

3. If not, are you willing to try to open your heart and allow yourself to be accepted?

4. Have you ever accepted Jesus Christ as your Savior and the restorer of your relationship with God? If not, would you like to? If so, turn to the **Acting on the Truth** section of Lesson 12 and read numbers 2, 3 and 4 which will help you work through this decision.

5. Are you willing to learn how to depend on God to meet your needs?

6. Do you realize your pain is normal?

7. Continue transforming your mind with God's truth by memorizing Romans 8:31, "*If God is for us, who can be against us?*" Each time you say it, spend time thinking about what it means for you and your situation.
8. Continue transforming your mind with God's truth by memorizing Romans 15:7 where it says, "*Accept one another, then, just as Christ accepted you, in order to bring praise to God.*" Each time you say it, spend time thinking about what it means for you and your situation.
9. Continue transforming your mind with God's truth by memorizing John 10:28,29 where Jesus said, "*...no one can snatch them out of my hand. My Father, who has given them to Me, is greater than all; no one can snatch them out of My Father's hand.*" Each time you say it, spend time thinking about what it means for you and your situation.

Transforming Benefits

1. **Rebuilding trust with others.** By realizing you are accepted by H.O.P.E., you can start to rebuild (or build) trust which will ultimately enable you to re-establish (or establish) relationships. However, the difference for your future will be that by

continuing to transform your mind each week with the truth, you will be able to do this in an emotionally healthy manner.

2. **Rebuilding trust with God.** By realizing God accepts you, you can start to rebuild (or build) trust with Him, which will ultimately enable you to re-establish (or establish) a relationship with Him. As a personal God, He is the only one who can provide acceptance and security for personal beings like us.
3. **Continue transforming your mind by dwelling on God's truth.** By memorizing the scripture verses, you will begin filling your mind and heart with God's Truth. You are what you think. Proverbs 23:7 says, "*For as he thinks within himself, so he is*" (NASV). What we think about and dwell on will affect our feelings, which in turn affects our attitudes, which ultimately, affects our behavior. You can begin to transform all of these by spending increasing amounts of time thinking about truth. By memorizing and focusing on the truth in the verses that prove you are accepted, you can change how you think about your life and your status in relation to your painful situation.

Truth 1: We All Experience Emotional Pain

"In this world you will have trouble. But take heart!
I have overcome the world."
(John 16:33)

You Are Loved

"For I am convinced that neither death nor life, neither angels nor demons, neither the present nor the future, nor any powers, neither height nor depth, nor anything else in all creation, will be able to separate us from the love of God that is in Christ Jesus our Lord."
(Romans 8:38,39)

Why Are You Here?

In Lesson 2 we discussed the **Three Truths About Life:**

1. We all live through painful experiences that can cause emotional wounds (some of which can be hidden).
2. Emotional wounds take longer to heal than physical wounds, but they can still be healed.
3. Jesus Christ wants to heal your emotional wounds.

In Lesson 3, we looked at Truth Number 1 more closely and elaborated on the encouragement that we can find in this truth. As we said:

Regardless of the number or severity of your emotional wounds, you are not alone.

Last week we discussed more encouraging news from this truth when we explained that you are accepted by God and by H.O.P.E. We discussed how acceptance is one of the two factors involved in meeting your need for security.

This week we will discuss more encouraging news from this truth as we focus on the other factor involved in meeting your need for security, namely love.

As we already said, just knowing that you are not alone is encouraging, but it is not enough. The same thing is true of acceptance. To know you are accepted is also encouraging, but not enough. You can be accepted into unhealthy environments, too, that fail to provide the necessary truth and compassion to succeed. You may have heard it said that there is even a code of honor among thieves.

To feel secure, you not only need to be accepted but you also need to be loved. You need to be accepted in a place where they love you enough to tell you the truth in a setting of mercy and compassion.

The third encouragement we want to share from Truth Number 1 is:

You are loved, both by God and by H.O.P.E.

Let's first discuss the truth that God loves you. In the struggles and pain of life, one of the biggest and most important questions you need answered is, "Does God really love me?" To help you understand the truth about the answer to this question, let's look at three ways that God shows His love for you. The three ways are:

1. He loves you enough to reveal Himself to you.
2. He loves you enough to relate to you.
3. He loves you enough to never repeal His love.

1. He loves you enough to reveal Himself to you

There are three ways God has shown His love for us by revealing Himself to us. He reveals Himself to us:

i. **Through creation** – Romans 1:19-20 says, "*...since what may be known about God is plain to them, because God has made it plain to them. For since the creation of the world God's invisible qualities—His eternal power and divine nature—have been clearly seen, being understood from what has been made, so that men are without excuse.*"

When you examine the universe, the human body or all the varieties in life (e.g. colors, species, tastes and smells) you can clearly see that God is organized, creative and intelligent. This topic will actually be addressed in more detail in the Level 2 *Names of H.O.P.E* group.

ii. **Through our experiences in life** – Whether we realize it yet or not, all of us can look back on times in our lives when God revealed Himself to us. We can see this in things that have happened (e.g. getting the new job or promotion, friends we have, having food to eat, etc.) and in things that did not happen (e.g. an accident that almost happened, a report coming back about a health condition we do not have, a relationship we were better off without, etc.).

iii. **Through Jesus Christ** – Jesus is the ultimate revelation of God to us because it was a personal revelation. To directly communicate to us, He became one of us. He also became the focal point of history in this revelation (He split time between A.D. and B.C.). Luke 2:32 says about Jesus that, "*He is a light to reveal God to the nations...*" (NLT). Colossians 1:15 says that, "*Christ is the visible image of the invisible God*" (NLT).

2. **<u>He loves you enough to relate to you</u>**

Not only did He reveal Himself to us as Jesus Christ, the reason Jesus came to earth was to die for us. His death was necessary to reestablish a relationship with us, since the effects of sin caused a separation from Him that needed to be bridged.

He did this even though He saw you as you really are. Romans 5:8 says, "*But God demonstrates His own love for us in this: While we were still sinners, Christ died for us.*" Philippians 2:6-8 says that Jesus, "*...Who, being in very nature God, did not consider equality with God something to be grasped, but made Himself nothing, taking the very nature of a servant, being made in human likeness. And being found in appearance as a man, He humbled Himself and became obedient to death—even death on a cross!*"

Now, because of His death, you can have both a relationship with God and you can receive His gift of eternal life. John 3:16 says, "*For God so loved the world, that He gave His one and only Son, that whoever believes in Him shall not perish but have eternal life.*"

His love is so great that He took the initiative in establishing a way for us to have a relationship with Him. As we said in the last lesson, this is a concept we will continue to discuss in more detail throughout this book (with particular emphasis in Lesson 12) and in the Level 2 *Names of H.O.P.E* group.

3. **<u>He loves you enough to never repeal His love</u>**

God will never revoke, cancel, retract, withdraw or remove His love for you. Psalm 136:6 states that, "*...His love endures forever.*" He actually cannot because the Bible says He is true love. He is the very essence of love, as it says in 1 John 4:8, "*...God is love.*"

Because of this, there is nothing you can do to make Him love you more and nothing you can do to make Him love you less. Nothing that you may have done or may have happened to you has any bearing on His love for you. He loves you right now in the midst of it all because His love is great enough to cover it all.

In Ephesians 3:18, Paul was praying that they would have the, "*...power, together with all the saints, to grasp how wide and long and high and deep is the love of Christ.*" Again in Romans 8:35,38,39 he wrote about how there is absolutely nothing that can separate us from His love when he said, "*Who shall separate us from the love of Christ? Shall trouble or hardship or persecution or famine or nakedness or danger or sword?...For I am convinced that neither death nor life, neither angels nor demons, neither the present nor the future, nor any powers, neither height nor depth, nor anything else in all creation, will be able to separate us from the love of God that is in Christ Jesus our Lord.*"

What this means is that on your worst day, in your worst circumstance, in your worst pain, in your worst suffering, you ***cannot*** be separated from the love of God in Jesus Christ.

In order for you to be able to fully grab a hold of this truth, it is critical for you to understand that love is ***not*** an emotion; love is a decision. It is a choice to always be there for someone, never leaving them or forsaking them. Love is a commitment to always do the right thing for someone, to always do what is best for them. Love is a promise to always take care of someone's spiritual, emotional and physical needs. To love someone means that they are safe, secure and protected with you. To love someone means to share your life with them in an environment that overflows with truth, peace, joy and happiness. In 1 Corinthians 13:8 it says, "*Love never fails.*"

Love also means teaching and preparing someone for life by instructing them in the truth, sharing wisdom with them and encouraging them along their journey. In 1 Corinthians 8:1

we read, *"...love builds up."* This means that when necessary, love also includes disciplining and forgiving those you love. But in all these things, it also means treating them the way God wants you to treat them, with compassion, mercy, patience and kindness. In 1 Corinthians 13:4 the Bible says, *"Love is patient, love is kind."*

As you can hopefully see from what was just described, love is not a noun. Love is a verb. It is an action word. Love is only love if it is expressed in word ***and*** deed. In 1 John 3:18 it says, *"Dear children, let us not love with words or tongue but with actions and in truth."* To love means giving of oneself sacrificially, to the point where you would die for those you love if need be. In John 15:13 Jesus said, *"Greater love has no one than this, that he lay down his life for his friends."* In 1 John 3:16 the Bible also says, *"This is how we know what love is: Jesus Christ laid down his life for us. And we ought to lay down our lives for our brothers."*

If you turn back to the three ways God shows His love for us, you will find that this true definition of love is exactly how God loves us. God made a decision to love us and He is committed to it. He has promised us that He will always be there for us, He will always do what is best for us, He will always provide for all our needs, He will keep us safe and secure, He will be our joy and peace, He will never fail us, He will instruct us and guide us, He will discipline us and forgive us, and He will treat us with compassion, mercy, patience and kindness. There is abundant ***action*** in God's love for us.

But since love is not an emotion, the feelings may not always be there. Right now you may be experiencing pain and suffering in your life and you do not "feel" like God loves you. But as we just clarified, love cannot be based on feelings. Plus, if you read through the definition of love we just provided, you will also see that there are parts of love that can actually be painful.

For example, instruction and discipline can be uncomfortable and they can hurt. But how they feel has no bearing on the fact that they are a part of love, they are a part of being committed to always doing what is best for someone else while guiding them through life. They are a part of loving someone too much to leave them where they are and wanting to bring them to a better place.

That is why, in addition to God's love for you, we also want you to know that you are loved here, too. We are here to put action to our love, too, by helping guide you through the pain of life. We do not want to see you remain where you are in your pain, either. We want to help bring you to a better place by enabling and empowering you to experience a transformed life.

We liken this ministry to a family. As we read in 1 Peter 3:8, "*...be sympathetic, love as brothers, be compassionate and humble.*" We are able to show you love because we, too, were shown love and now it is become a calling for us. As the Bible says in 1 John 3:11, "*This is the message you heard from the beginning: We should love one another.*"

We love you enough to share the truth with you and we strive to do that in a compassionate manner. In Ephesians 4:15 we read, "*...speaking the truth in love, we will in all things grow up into Him who is the Head, that is, Christ.*" Later in that same chapter of Ephesians we also read, "*Be kind and compassionate to one another*" (Ephesians 4:32).

Truth

No matter how you may feel today, the truth is that God really loves you and truly cares about everything you are experiencing. If God had a refrigerator, He would have ***your*** picture on it because ***He is crazy about you!***

Lesson 3 includes some of my testimony in which God provided for me in personal and specific ways (and hopefully you also heard a testimony from your group leader during that lesson). I included this information so you would know that God is a God who cares in personal and specific ways.

It is very important to mention that God's personal and specific care is available to all of us, including ***you!*** No matter what your situation is or what your needs are, God truly cares about everything in your life because He cares about ***you!*** The beautiful aspect of God's care is that He does not ***just*** care. He cares so much that He will step in and do something to provide for your situation and needs, to the point of performing a miracle if that is what is necessary.

The reason God cares about you is because He loves you. God loves you because you are valuable and worthwhile to Him. Think about that for a minute, you are valuable and worthwhile to the Creator of the Universe! As we learned in this lesson, love is only love if it is expressed in word and deed. There must be action in love because love is a verb. If you allow God to fill you with His love, you will discover that there is ***abundant*** action in His love for you.

Love is one of the key ingredients (along with acceptance) necessary for all of us to meet one of our two basic needs, the need for security. This is such a strong need in our lives that we will take great risks to pursue it. Unfortunately, our pursuit often leads to many types of unhealthy behaviors in our relationships (e.g. dependencies or isolation). But none of these pursuits will ever meet this need.

As with acceptance, only a personal God can meet the personal need for love that we all have. He can provide all the love you need.

God loves you enough to reveal Himself to you with a love that is so great and powerful that nothing can separate you from it. That is because His love is based on who ***He*** is, not who ***you*** are. God even died for you as proof of His great love for you. As Jesus said in John 15:13, *"Greater love has no one than this, that he lay down his life for his friends."*

As a result of this act of love, you can now be called His friend. This will give you the confidence to answer "Yes" to the critical question you will likely ask in the midst of your suffering, "Does God really love me?" You have His Word on it.

In addition, those of us at H.O.P.E. are here out of a love for you, too. We will do everything we can to foster an environment where you can truly feel that love. We love you enough to share the truth with you out of our compassion for you. In 1 John 3:18 it says, *"Dear children, let us not love with words or tongue but with actions and in truth."* We are able to do this for you because others have previously done it for us.

Checking In

Take a minute to review the **Guidelines for Checking In** found in Lesson 1.

Please use this time today to talk about anything you are comfortable with sharing. You can share what has been happening lately in your life or how you feel about what we just discussed. Regardless of the issue, focus on how you feel about it and how it is affecting you.

A good way to get started is by telling the people in your group about how you handled and answered the items from last week's **Acting on the Truth** section. Or maybe you might want to tell them if any of the items were particularly difficult to deal with or hard to understand. You may also tell them if any of the things we just discussed are difficult for you to understand or accept.

At the completion of your time, we would like you to say, "I'm in" signifying that your time is completed. If you do not want to share this week, that is fine. But we still require you to at least say, "I'm in."

To help you get started, you may want to address the following statements and questions:

1. Briefly introduce yourself.
2. Why are you here and what expectations do you have from this ministry?
3. Have you been in a group like this before and what was it like?
4. How do you feel about being here?

Acting On The Truth

1. How have you pursued love and security from other people?

____

____

____

____

2. Do you realize yet that Jesus loves you so much He died for you? Have you ever responded to His love by accepting Jesus Christ as your Savior? If not, would you like to? If so, turn to the **Acting on the Truth** section of Lesson 12 and read numbers 2, 3 and 4 which will help you work through this decision.

____

3. Are you willing to try to open your heart and allow yourself to be loved by God and by H.O.P.E.?

____

4. Continue transforming your mind with God's truth by memorizing John 3:16, *"For God so loved the world, that He gave His one and only Son, that whoever believes in Him shall not perish but have eternal life."* Each time you say it, spend time thinking about what it means for you and your situation.
5. Continue transforming your mind with God's truth by memorizing Psalm 136:6, *"...His love endures forever."* Each time you say it, spend time thinking about what it means for you and your situation.

Transforming Benefits

1. **Rebuilding trust with others.** By realizing you are loved by H.O.P.E., you can feel secure enough to start to rebuild (or build) trust which will ultimately enable you to re-establish (or establish) relationships. However, the difference for your future will be that by continuing to transform your mind each week with the truth, you will be able to do this in an emotionally healthy manner.
2. **Rebuilding trust with God.** By realizing God loves you, you can feel secure enough to start to rebuild (or build) trust with Him, which will ultimately enable you to re-establish (or establish) a relationship with Him. As a personal God, He is the only one who can provide love and security for personal beings like us.
3. **Relating to God.** When you accept that God loves you so much that He died for you to take away the penalty for your sins, you can begin life anew as a child of God. This means that you have the gift of eternal life plus the gift of a better life here and now with your personal Lord, Savior and friend, Jesus Christ.
4. **Continue transforming your mind by dwelling on God's truth.** By memorizing the scripture verses, you will begin filling your mind and heart with God's Truth. You are what you think. Proverbs 23:7 says, "*For as he thinks within himself, so he is*" (NASV). What we think about and dwell on will affect our feelings, which in turn affects our attitudes, which ultimately, affects our behavior. You can begin to transform all of these by spending increasing amounts of time thinking about truth. By memorizing and focusing on the truth in the verses that prove you are loved, you can change how you think about your life and your status in relation to your painful situation.

Truth 1: We All Experience Emotional Pain

"In this world you will have trouble. But take heart!
I have overcome the world."
(John 16:33)

Lesson 6

It is OK To Talk About It

"I must speak and find relief..."
(Job 32:20)

Why Are You Here?

In Lesson 2 we discussed the **Three Truths About Life:**

1. We all live through painful experiences that can cause emotional wounds (some of which can be hidden).
2. Emotional wounds take longer to heal than physical wounds, but they can still be healed.
3. Jesus Christ wants to heal your emotional wounds.

In Lesson 3, we looked at Truth Number 1 more closely and elaborated on the encouragement that we can find in this truth. As we said:

Regardless of the number or severity of your emotional wounds, you are not alone.

In Lessons 4 and 5, we discussed more encouraging news from this truth when we explained that you are accepted and loved by God and by H.O.P.E. We discussed how acceptance and love are the two factors involved in meeting your need for security.

This week we will discuss more encouraging news from this truth. We will focus on:

> ***How feeling secure can give you the power to take the first step in adopting a healthy approach to dealing with your pain.***

This approach can lead to beneficial, transforming changes in your life.

> *Leading Question:* How many of you here are in the category of those who are taking a ***healthy*** approach to dealing with their pain? How is that approach working for you?

This ministry is full of people like that. The one thing that each and every one of us has in common is that we all took the first healthy step in dealing with our pain:

> ***We realized and accepted the truth that it is OK to talk about it with other people who care enough about you to share the truth with you.***

The first step in dealing with your pain in a healthy manner and transforming your life is:

> ***Accepting the truth that it is OK to talk about it.***

The second part of this truth is equally as important:

> ***You need to find a safe place to talk about it, one where people care enough about you to tell you the truth.***

Unless you fully grasp this concept and recognize it to be true, most of us will instead believe the lie that proclaims us to be outcasts because of our situation in life. This forces us into pursuing a lifestyle where we do all we can to hide the truth of our pain. The tragedy of such a lifestyle is that it only results in alienating ourselves from the truth, from the pathway to healing and freedom, from others and from God.

In the movie "Shrek", when we first meet Shrek he is in a situation where he had chosen to believe the lie that said he was nothing more than a smelly old ogre.

> Leading Question: How many of you have seen Shrek? Did you like the movie? Did you realize there was a message in the movie about emotional health?

Shrek chose to live in a way that alienated himself from everyone and everything to try to hide his pain. But the truth of his pain begins to appear after he meets Donkey.

Donkey, with his incessant barrage of dialogue, forces Shrek to talk about his pain and get it out in the open. At one point, Shrek tries to explain that he has emotional layers, like an onion. But Donkey quickly and relentlessly forces Shrek to see the truth of how he has wrapped himself up so tightly in his layers that he has used them as a wall to keep everyone and everything out, including the truth.

Donkey says to Shrek at one point, "You're so wrapped up in your layers, onion boy, that you cannot see the truth!"

Here is the point. Your emotions were not meant to be a wall of separation, they were meant to be a doorway to fellowship and community.

> ***Your emotions were meant to be shared.***

I believe that the reason our tears flow down on the ***outside*** of our face and not on the inside through our sinuses where they would not be seen is because it is a reminder for us to share our pain.

Ecclesiastes 3:7 says that there is, "*...a time to be silent and a time to speak...*" When we are in pain, it is ***not*** a time to be silent. It is a time to speak. Keeping silent and trying to keep it hidden inside will only make matters worse and ultimately lead to disaster.

David learned this truth the hard way, as we find from Psalm 32:3 where he wrote, "*When I kept silent, my bones wasted away through my groaning all day long.*" In Psalm 39:2 he also wrote, "*But when I was silent and still, not even saying anything good, my anguish increased.*"

Jeremiah also understood the futility of trying to keep his pain inside, as we learn from Jeremiah 4:19 where he wrote, "*Oh, my anguish, my anguish! I writhe in pain. Oh, the agony of my heart! My heart pounds within me, I cannot keep silent.*"

Elihu was a young man who was greatly troubled by the conversations between Job and his three friends found in chapters 3-31 of the book of Job. Rather than keep his feelings inside, Elihu answers Job and his three friends in Job 32:20 by saying, "*I must speak and find relief; I must open my lips and reply.*" Later in Job 34:4 he also says, "*Let us discern for ourselves what is right; let us learn together what is good.*"

From these verses we learn that Elihu knew that it was emotionally healthy to share his feelings and not keep them inside where they would be able to fester. He knew that the best way to work through those feelings and find the truth was by sharing them.

In Mark 4:22 Jesus said, "*For whatever is hidden is meant to be disclosed, and whatever is concealed is meant to be brought out into the open.*" When He spoke these words, Jesus was primarily referring to spreading the Good News of the kingdom of God. But He was also teaching us a Biblical principle in how to handle our emotional pain in a healthy manner. Pain was never meant to be concealed, it was meant to be shared.

This principle not only applies to the emotional pain we try to hide, but also to the unhealthy and sinful ways that we try to cope with our pain. Proverbs 28:13 says, "*He who conceals his sins does not prosper, but whoever confesses and renounces them finds mercy.*" James 5:16 also says, "*Therefore confess your sins to each other and pray for each other so that you may be healed. The prayer of a righteous man is powerful and effective.*"

Admitting your pain by opening up and sharing it is not a sign of weakness or illness, it is a sign of health and wholeness. It opens us up to access the one true source of help in overcoming our pain.

In 2 Corinthians 12:9, the apostle Paul wrote about how God answered his questions about his own weakness by saying, "*But He said to me, 'My grace is sufficient for you, for My power is made perfect in weakness.' Therefore I will boast all the more gladly about my weaknesses, so that Christ's power may rest on me.*'"

By learning the truth that it is OK to talk about our pain, we can find strength in the care, support and encouragement of God. Psalm 68:19 says, "*Praise be to the Lord, to God our Savior, who daily bears our burdens.*" We can also find strength in the care, support and encouragement of others. We read this in 1 Thessalonians 5:11 where it says, "*Therefore encourage one another and build each other up.*"

We are all here because we want to help. But not only that, it is a calling for us. In Galatians 6:2 the Bible says, "*Bear one another's burdens, and thereby fulfill the law of Christ*"

(NASV). That is one of the main reasons we are here, to help bear the pain and burdens of those who are hurting.

Therefore, we will do everything we can to foster an environment that makes you feel safe enough to share your pain. However, we know that this is an extremely difficult concept for some. So to be clear:

> ***We are not here to force you to open up and talk about it.***

As we read in Ephesians 4:2, *"Be completely humble and gentle; be patient, bearing with one another in love."*

Rather:

> ***We are here to create an environment that makes you feel safe enough to lower your walls of isolation and want to share your pain.***

That is what ***Doorway to H.O.P.E.*** **Guideline number 1** is all about. So let's look at that guideline now. The guideline states:

> ***Safety.*** Our objective is to make our groups a place where we can feel safe to be vulnerable. Members will need to determine their own safety zones and what goes beyond those zones. The goal is to have everyone feel safe enough to expand those comfort zones as time elapses.

Guidelines 2, the **Confidentiality Guideline** (which we take very seriously), 6, the **First Person Focus Guideline** and 7, the **No Disruptions Guideline**, (which are the two that help us maintain our focus on you and help you without going down rabbit trails) are also necessary to create this type of environment.

Some people in our groups will be ready for this right now and want to open up immediately. If that is you, then we applaud you.

The difference you will hopefully find by sharing your pain with us is that we care enough about you to tell you the truth. We are here to provide you with the support you need to make healthy choices and healthy changes.

Once you are at a place where you want to share your pain, you must be discerning with whom you choose to share. Choosing the wrong audience can lead to unhealthy feedback and end up causing more damage.

At the same time, some of you may not be ready to open up yet. If that is you, we want to say as plainly as we can, "That's OK."

As time passes, we hope that you will eventually feel safe enough and develop enough trust in this group to be ready at a future date. Many people in this ministry have experienced the same thing and can tell you that it is worth the effort to share once you come to that place.

And some of you may be somewhere in between. When you are at the place where you are somewhat comfortable with opening up and sharing, we do not expect you to share everything at once.

As the guideline states, if you are trying to share one week but start feeling uncomfortable, it is OK to stop. Do not feel forced to continue immediately if you find yourself getting uncomfortable. It is OK to stop and try again next week. This is just like any other skill we learn in life, the more you actually do it, the more comfortable you become and the easier it is to do in the future.

This all points to a concept you will learn throughout all our programs:

> ***The journey toward wholeness and healing is a marathon, not a sprint, that happens one day at a time.***

To break this down even further, the journey toward wholeness and healing happens one hour at a time, or even one moment at a time. Each positive and healthy step you make will build upon the previous ones and add up over time. As the old proverb says, "A journey of a thousand miles begins with a single step."

Truth

God intended for you to share your pain. No matter what lies you may have learned previously in life, it is OK to share how you are hurting.

Not only that, but it is the healthy and mature thing to do. Learning to open up and talk about it is a positive step. The alternative will cause your emotions to remain trapped and the results can be disastrous.

Let us illustrate this for you.

> Leader's Note: If one is available, it may be helpful to draw this illustration on a chalkboard or whiteboard. You can do so by simply drawing two circles connected by a line. In one circle, write "Time and Sequence" to represent the sensory cortex and in the other circle write "Feelings and Emotions" to represent the amygdala. As you discuss how inappropriately handling your feelings blocks this connection, you can draw an arrow pointing to the line you drew between the two circles.

The brain has two separate areas that deal with feelings/emotions (mainly in the amygdala) and time/sequence (mainly in the sensory cortex). In order to appropriately handle your feelings, the sensory information gets routed from the amygdala via the thalamus to the sensory cortex, where it can be synchronized, made sense of, appropriately perceived and resolved. However, if you do not take the initial steps to open up and talk about them, your feelings and emotions will get stuck in time. The result of this is that your brain will not be able to process your feelings properly.

To be clear, understanding the names of the brain here is not what is important. What is important is to understand that by ***not*** talking about your feelings and emotions and suppressing them, you are blocking the connection in these two areas of the brain.

Trying to block this connection in your brain can be very costly. In essence, it is like trying to hold back the water from a fire hydrant with a garden hose. The water pressure inside a fire hydrant will eventually burst the garden hose and cause it to erupt.

In the same way, the emotional pressure built up by not talking about your pain will eventually cause you to erupt. This clearly illustrates the principle:

What we do not talk out constructively, we will act out destructively.

As you can see from this illustration, believing that it is better not to talk about it can have tragic consequences. Maybe that is just what you were told. You may have been told not to talk about it, or to ignore it, or that it is really not that bad, etc. Feedback from our history and experiences that is based on lies, whether intentional or unintentional, will only cause more harm and keep your emotional health in bondage.

If this is you, you need to come to the place where you start acting on the truth instead of the lies. You also need to recognize that you need a safe, healthy and truthful environment in which to do that. Truthful feedback from people who honestly care about you will promote positive changes that can help to transform your life and enable you to grow. As God tells us in Zechariah 7:9, "*...show mercy and compassion to one another.*"

Hopefully, you will find that to be true in this ministry. We are here because we honestly care about the pain you are experiencing. The reason is simple. We care because we, too, have lived through pain. Yet someone cared enough about us to tell us God's truth and help us overcome our pain.

So now, out of gratitude for the help and the truth we have received, we want to turn around and pass it along. As we also read in Lesson 3, once again 2 Corinthians 1:3-4 says, "*Blessed be the God and Father of our Lord Jesus Christ, the Father of mercies and God of all comfort; who comforts us in all our afflictions so that we may be able to comfort those who are in any affliction with the comfort with which we ourselves are comforted by God*" (NASV).

Checking In

Take a minute to review the **Guidelines for Checking In** found in Lesson 1.

Please use this time today to talk about anything you are comfortable with sharing. You can share what has been happening lately in your life or how you feel about what we just discussed. Regardless of the issue, focus on how you feel about it and how it is affecting you.

A good way to get started is by telling the people in your group about how you handled and answered the items from last week's **Acting on the Truth** section. Or maybe you might want to tell them if any of the items were particularly difficult to deal with or hard to understand. You may also tell them if any of the things we just discussed are difficult for you to understand or accept.

At the completion of your time, we would like you to say, "I'm in" signifying that your time is completed. If you do not want to share this week, that is fine. But we still require you to at least say, "I'm in."

To help you get started, you may want to address the following statements and questions:

1. Briefly introduce yourself.
2. Why are you here and what expectations do you have from this ministry?
3. Have you been in a group like this before and what was it like?
4. How do you feel about being here?

Acting on the Truth

1. How do you feel about sharing your pain?

____

____

____

____

2. What have you been taught about sharing your pain and feelings?

____

____

____

____

3. Are you willing to begin trusting in the truth about sharing your feelings and pain?

____

4. Begin transforming your mind with God's truth by memorizing 2 Corinthians 12:9, *"But He said to me, 'My grace is sufficient for you, for my power is made perfect in weakness.' Therefore I will boast all the more gladly about my weaknesses, so that Christ's power may rest on me.'"* Each time you say it, spend time thinking about what it means for you and your situation.
5. Continue transforming your mind with God's truth by memorizing Job 32:20, *"I must speak and find relief..."* Each time you say it, spend time thinking about what it means for you and your situation.
6. Continue transforming your mind with God's truth by memorizing Psalm 68:19, *"Praise be to the Lord, to God our Savior, who daily bears our burdens."* Each time you say it, spend time thinking about what it means for you and your situation.

Transforming Benefits

1. **Unclogging your emotional back up.** Talking about it is the first step toward releasing all the emotional pressure that has built up in your life. Talking about it in a healthy environment is both a safe and effective way to begin to experience the freedom of overcoming emotional pain. It will enable you to appropriately process and handle your feelings in a way that will lead to a healthy resolution.
2. **Continue transforming your mind by dwelling on God's truth.** By memorizing the scripture verses, you will begin filling your mind and heart with God's Truth. You are what you think. Proverbs 23:7 says, "*For as he thinks within himself, so he is*" (NASV). What we think about and dwell on will affect our feelings, which in turn affects our attitudes, which ultimately, affects our behavior. You can begin to transform all of these by spending increasing amounts of time thinking about truth. By memorizing and focusing on the truth in the verses that prove how God designed us to share our pain, you can begin to change how you feel about what to do with your emotional pain.
3. **Physical relief.** By getting your pain "off your chest" and out in the open where it is safe and can be dealt with, you will begin to feel physical relief from carrying around your burdens. You can begin to enjoy how it feels to have the weight of the world lifted from your shoulders.
4. **One day at a time.** By applying the principle of taking everything you do in this process one day at a time, one hour at a time or one moment at a time, you can begin to tackle the feelings of being overwhelmed. Each day focus only on what you need to do that day and leave tomorrow for tomorrow.

Truth 2: Emotional Wounds Can Be Healed

"He heals the brokenhearted and binds up their wounds."
(Psalm 147:3)

Lesson 7

You Cannot Heal Your Wounds By Saying They Are Not There

"My heart has heard you say, 'Come and talk with me.' And my heart responds, 'LORD, I am coming'" (NLT).
(Psalm 27:8)

Why Are You Here?

In Lesson 2 we discussed the **Three Truths About Life:**

1. We all live through painful experiences that can cause emotional wounds (some of which can be hidden).
2. Emotional wounds take longer to heal than physical wounds, but they can still be healed.
3. Jesus Christ wants to heal your emotional wounds.

In Lesson 3 we looked at Truth Number 1 more closely and elaborated on the encouragement that we can find in this truth. As we said:

> ***Regardless of the number or severity of your emotional wounds, you are <u>not</u> <u>alone</u>.***

In Lessons 4 through 6, we discussed more encouraging news from this truth when we explained that you are accepted and loved by God and by H.O.P.E. We discussed how acceptance and love are the two factors involved in meeting your need for security, and:

> ***How feeling secure can give you the power to take the first step in adopting a healthy approach to dealing with your pain.***

For the next four Lessons, we will look at Truth Number 2 more closely and elaborate on the encouragement that we can find in this truth. As we said in Lesson 2:

> ***Something <u>can</u> be done about your pain.***

Looking at Truth Number 2 we find that emotional wounds take longer to heal than physical wounds, but they can still be healed.

When we have a physical wound, there is a wonderful and miraculous process by which our body naturally repairs the damage. There is a cascade of events that allows our blood to clot and ***stop*** the bleeding, followed by another cascade of events that allows the damaged tissue to ***start*** to be revitalized.

Just as with physical wounds, there are also things we must both ***stop*** and ***start*** doing to allow the healing process to begin with our emotional wounds. Specifically, we must:

1. **<u>Stop</u>**
    a. Denying the pain and problems
    b. Playing God

2. **<u>Start</u>**
    a. Admitting your helplessness
    b. Admitting your situation is beyond your control

Let's look a little closer at what each of these means.

Stop denying the pain and problems

Denial has been defined as a false system of beliefs not based on reality, and self-protecting behavior that keeps us from honestly facing the truth. There is a cartoon that illustrates denial very well. A cow is lying on its back with all four legs sticking straight up in the air and its eyes are crossed out. But the caption for the cartoon reads, "Really, I'm fine!"

The "coping skills" of denial, like the one used by the cow, were learned to block our fears and pain, but they only lead to confusion and clouding of the truth. These coping skills come in many varieties, too. For example, do any of these sound familiar?

- Pretending things really are not so bad.
- Ignoring the issues and hoping they just go away.
- Substance abuse.
- Depression.
- An altered view of how you treat others and expect to be treated.
- Staying so busy that you avoid the issues.

> Leading Question: Think about the coping mechanisms we just mentioned or any others you have tried. I would like to ask you, "How's that working for you?"

These are just a few examples of the coping skills that many of us try. Sadly, the list goes on and on, as you may well know. Left alone, these coping skills are extremely harmful; unfortunately, we compound our pain our pain and emotional problems when we combine these denial mechanisms with any one of the three most destructive emotions: resentment, guilt and anxiety.

We will discuss the damage that these three emotions can cause in much more detail in future lessons and in the Level 2 *Names of H.O.P.E.* group, but for now it is important to note:

a. **Resentment** is very self-destructive and emotionally draining, as we read in Job 18:4, *"You who tear yourself to pieces in your anger..."*

b. **Guilt** is also incredibly destructive. It is the number one cause of low self-esteem and depression, and the most recent numbers show that 35 million adults in the U.S. suffer from depression.

c. **Anxiety** and worry are the result of **FEAR**, False Evidence Appearing Real, which is the most common harmful emotion. Fear mainly comes from not knowing the truth. Worry depletes your energy and exaggerates the problem. Psalm 25:17 says, *"The troubles of my heart are enlarged..."* (NASV). It wastes your time because worry has never solved a single problem and cannot add a single moment to your life. In Matthew 6:27 Jesus said, *"Who of you by worrying can add a single hour to his life?"*

These emotions trap your life in the past and/or the future while controlling your present.

Stop playing God

We have a member of this ministry who has become somewhat famous for a few of his quotes. One of them that he often repeats is, "God is God and I am not."

This is a simple, yet profound statement. A truth that is critical for you to understand. We are not God and so we cannot do His job. But we end up playing God when we try to handle the pain on our own. You have been trying to do God's job, but you cannot because it has never been your job to try to control or fix your pain. You do not hold God up; He holds you up.

Our attempts to do His job and control ourselves and others are what got us here in the first place. The more we try to control things, the more our "self" runs out of control. When your "self" is out of control, all attempts at control fail. You cannot serve yourself and God. In Matthew 6:24 Jesus said, *"No one can serve two masters..."*

Leading Question: Think about whether or not you have been trying to play God. If so, I would like to ask you, "How's that working for you?"

Start admitting your helplessness

We all need to realize that we are human and we all have weaknesses. When it comes to the pain in our lives, this is especially true. The lie is that we can take care of this by ourselves. But the truth is that we cannot. We need help. We need God's help. The sooner we admit we need help, the sooner we will quit trying to do it by ourselves and the sooner we can actually start receiving help.

Viewing our history of failure in this area can enable us to clearly focus on the fact that we do not have the power to take charge and change the things we thought we could change.

This is not an easy thing to do; in fact it can be rather difficult. Jesus knew this would be hard to do, which is why He encouraged us in Matthew 19:26 by saying, "*With man this is impossible, but with God all things are possible.*"

> Leading Question: If you have been thinking you are self-sufficient and can take care of this by yourself, I would just like to ask you, "How's that working for you?"

Start admitting your situation is beyond your control

This step goes hand in hand with the previous step. It is actually very freeing to admit that your situation is beyond your control. You have to get to this point before you will be willing to turn it over to someone else's control.

My two boys love to go to Chuck E. Cheese and play games. (Truth be told, so do I.) There is one game there called "Whack-A-Mole." Little moles keep popping up out of their holes and you have to smack them back down to score points. But as quickly as you smack one down, another one pops up. More moles just keep popping up, over and over again, no matter how many you smack down.

When we try to control our problems all by ourselves, we are living our lives like we are playing "Whack-A-Mole." The more we try to knock one issue down, the more other ones keep popping up.

Living like this will never work. This only produces the feeling of being overwhelmed, because the vast majority of our lives is beyond our control. Obviously, you cannot control what is beyond your control.

> Leading Question: Think about it, how much of your life can you actually control?

Although most of our life is out of our control, there is one thing we can always control, no matter what we experience and no matter how painful it is:

> ***We can always control how we respond to a situation (assuming we have the appropriate mental capacity).***

Believe it or not, an emotionally healthy response is one where you say, "I can't do this! I give up!" When you do, you are exactly where God's been waiting for you to be, because then He can say, "Finally! Now I can accomplish some things in your life!"

The healthy response is to give up your attempts at control and give it over to the Lord. Once you give control over to God, it then becomes ***His responsibility*** to resolve your troubles and pain. He has promised to help us in Isaiah 41:13 where it says, *"For I am the LORD, your God, who takes hold of your right hand and says to you, Do not fear; I will help you."*

> Leading Question: If you have been trying to control everything in your situation, I would like to ask you, "How's that working for you?"

Truth

As Truth 2 says, emotional wounds take longer to heal than physical wounds, but they can still be healed.

The first step to healing those wounds is to make some changes in how you have been trying to handle the pain. You need to stop denying the pain and the problem and stop playing God. You also need to start admitting you are helpless and that your situation is out of your control. You simply cannot begin the process of transforming your life until you do these things first.

We are sure this is both a new and a foreign concept to many of you. It may seem counter-intuitive, as well. It may also seem to be very difficult to accomplish.

If that is what you are thinking now, then you are correct on all counts. But we want to make it very clear that although it may seem impossible, it ***can*** be done. This ministry is full of people who can testify to that. The key is to utilize the support available to you to make it happen and to remember that "You do not help you; God helps you." Psalm 54:4 reads, *"Surely God is my help; the Lord is the one who sustains me."*

Positive change can only occur in the present, so you need to stop living in the past and/or dreading the future. You need to renew your mind with God's truth that clearly shows you a better way. You then need to choose to follow His way even though it may seem difficult and scary.

Fear is the main opposition to turning control over to God. But as we discussed in our previous lessons, God loves you and accepts you just as you are. Therefore, you need to allow this truth to sink in and overcome your fear by realizing that God is on your side and wants to help.

You need to admit to the reality of your situation so your wounds can begin to heal. You cannot begin the process of healing if you do not take this first step. As it says in Psalm 32:3, "*When I kept silent, my bones wasted away through my groaning all day long.*"

As an added incentive to overcoming your fear of taking this step, we want to reiterate that not only will God be there for you, but we will, too. We will help you every step of the way as you walk away from your coping skills and toward the truth. Please understand this truth, so you can let your pain outweigh your fear and choose to make a change.

Besides, what is the alternative? To keep living the way you have been living? How bad does it have to get before you do something about it? Finally, we ask you, "How's that been working for you?"

Checking In

Take a minute to review the **Guidelines for Checking In** found in Lesson 1.

Please use this time today to talk about anything you are comfortable with sharing. You can share what has been happening lately in your life or how you feel about what we just discussed. Regardless of the issue, focus on how you feel about it and how it is affecting you.

A good way to get started is by telling the people in your group about how you handled and answered the items from last week's **Acting on the Truth** section. Or maybe you might want to tell them if any of the items were particularly difficult to deal with or hard to understand. You may also tell them if any of the things we just discussed are difficult for you to understand or accept.

At the completion of your time, we would like you to say, "I'm in" signifying that your time is completed. If you do not want to share this week, that is fine. But we still require you to at least say, "I'm in."

To help you get started, you may want to address the following statements and questions:

1. Briefly introduce yourself.
2. Why are you here and what expectations do you have from this ministry?
3. Have you been in a group like this before and what was it like?
4. How do you feel about being here?

Acting on the Truth

1. What coping skills have you used, or continue to use, to escape pain?

____

____

____

____

2. What areas of your life can you control? What areas can you not control?

____

____

____

____

3. Do you spend a lot of time worrying and dealing with anxiety? What are you afraid of?

____

____

____

____

4. Do you need help getting your life back under control?

____

5. Continue transforming your mind with God's truth by memorizing Psalm 147:3, *"He heals the brokenhearted and binds up their wounds."* Each time you say it, spend time thinking about what it means for you and your situation.
6. Continue transforming your mind with God's truth by memorizing Psalm 54:4, *"Surely God is my help; the LORD is the one who sustains me."* Each time you say it, spend time thinking about what it means for you and your situation.

Transforming Benefits

1. **Taking the first step towards positive change.** When you stop denying the pain, stop playing God and start admitting your helplessness and that your situation is beyond your control, you take the first step towards a transformed life. Your journey cannot begin until you honestly take this first step.
2. **Learning to trust in God and overcome your fears.** Positive change can only occur in the present, so you need to stop living in the past and/or dreading the future. Holding on to pain from the past or fear of the future only allows it to continue hurting you in the present. When your pain is greater than your fear, you are ready to start making changes. By stepping out of your denial mechanisms and fear and into the truth, you also begin the process of learning to trust God with your life. It does not matter if this is the first time you are doing this or the hundredth, God can still be trusted to help you overcome your pain and restore you to wholeness.
3. **Better preparing yourself to handle your current pain.** Like preparing for war, you must know what you are facing before you can develop a plan of attack. As it has been said, "A problem well defined is a problem half solved."
4. **Better preparing yourself to handle pain in the future.** When you realize you need to talk about your pain and honestly deal with it here and now, you will begin learning how to better prepare yourself for troubles in the future. By seeing your situations as they really are and opening up about them sooner than later in a safe environment, you can prevent situations in the future from getting out of control.
5. **Peace of mind.** Peace of mind comes from the assurance that when you turn control over to the Lord, it now becomes His responsibility and you are free from the frustration of trying to maintain control. We will discuss peace more in Lesson 9.
6. **Continue transforming your mind by dwelling on God's truth.** By memorizing the scripture verses, you will begin filling your mind and heart with God's Truth. You are what you think. Proverbs 23:7 says, "*For as he thinks within himself, so he is*" (NASV). What we think about and dwell on will affect our feelings, which in turn affects our attitudes, which ultimately, affects our behavior. You can begin to transform all of these by spending increasing amounts of time thinking about truth. By memorizing and focusing on the truth in the verses that prove how you need to step out of your coping mechanisms, you can change how you think about the status of your life in relation to your painful situation.

Truth 2: Emotional Wounds Can Be Healed

"He heals the brokenhearted and binds up their wounds."
(Psalm 147:3)

Lesson 8

You Need Your Wounds To Be Healed

"'For I know the plans I have for you,' declares the LORD,
'plans to prosper you and not to harm you,
plans to give you hope and a future.'"
(Jeremiah 29:11)

Why Are You Here?

In Lesson 2 we discussed the **Three Truths About Life:**

1. We all live through painful experiences that can cause emotional wounds (some of which can be hidden).
2. Emotional wounds take longer to heal than physical wounds, but they can still be healed.
3. Jesus Christ wants to heal your emotional wounds.

In Lesson 3 we looked at Truth Number 1 more closely and elaborated on the encouragement that we can find in this truth. As we said:

> ***Regardless of the number or severity of your emotional wounds, you are not alone.***

In Lessons 4 through 6, we discussed more encouraging news from this truth when we explained that you are accepted and loved by God and by H.O.P.E. We discussed how acceptance and love are the two factors involved in meeting your need for security, and:

> ***How feeling secure can give you the power to take the first step in adopting a healthy approach to dealing with your pain.***

Last week, we looked at Truth Number 2 more closely and elaborated on the encouragement that we can find in this truth. As we said:

> ***Something can be done about your pain.***

Last week, we also discussed how you need to stop denying your pain, stop playing God and start admitting you are helpless and your situation is beyond your control.

This week, we will continue discussing this encouragement from Truth Number 2 by focusing on why you need your emotional wounds healed:

> ***You need your emotional wounds healed in order to start living the life of fullness that God intended you to live.***

Let's begin with a story. There was a father who had a hard week at work and he was tired. After church on Sunday, he was really hoping to take a nap.

But his son had different ideas. It was a beautiful day and he wanted to go outside and play baseball. So while his father was reading the paper, he asked, "Dad, can we go outside and play ball?" The father knew when he heard this question that his plan to take a nap was in serious jeopardy.

But as he was looking through the paper, he came across an insert that gave him hope. The insert was a puzzle of the world, with many of the countries cut into puzzle pieces. Knowing that his son was still too young to have had any classes in geography, he told him, "We can go outside and play after you put this puzzle of the world together."

He gave his son the puzzle pieces and went off to take his nap knowing it would be quite awhile before his son figured out the puzzle.

But after only a few minutes, his son came to him and said, "Dad, I'm done. Can we go outside and play now?" His dad was shocked and asked him, "How did you do that so fast?" His son replied, "There was a cartoon of a person on the other side, so I just turned all the pieces over and put the puzzle together that way.

Here is the point of this story:

When you get your "person" right, the whole world looks much better.

When our lives and our very selves are "out of whack", our entire outlook on life will be distorted. Unfortunately, when emotional pain enters our lives it very often causes us to fall out of emotional and spiritual alignment. We can no longer maintain a healthy perspective on any of the aspects of our lives.

Sadly, many people can remain trapped in this lie for the rest of their lives.

Recently my wife and I were having a lunch date at a local restaurant. When we got up to leave, they were playing a song that I did not recognize, but one line of the song really caught my attention. The line went, "Does anybody else here feel like they're only half alive?"

After hearing that I thought, "How sad that is, but yet, how true." The song pointed out a heartbreaking fact about our world today; most people never really live, they just exist.

Like a person who needs to visit a chiropractor when their back is out of alignment, we need to get our emotional and spiritual health back into alignment with the truth in God's Word. We need to do this so we can learn how to really live and avoid merely existing. We need to stand up and start living the way God intended us to live.

In order to do that, you must first realize that your life is worth living. As a member of a group of people in this ministry who have been there and lived to tell about it, we can honestly say from experience that each and every life is worth living, including yours. We want to say this as clearly as we can:

You are worthwhile!

To be able to fully realize this, you need to grab a hold of the truth that ***God*** thinks you are worthwhile. He has a better life for you that is worth living. Jesus said in John 10:10, *"The thief comes only to steal and kill and destroy; I have come that they may have life, and have it to the full."*

If you continue to live your life based on lies that say your life is not worth it and you do not deserve any better, you will never get beyond merely existing. That is because:

To feel worthwhile is the most basic of all needs that we have in life.

There are two ingredients necessary for meeting this need. As we discussed in Lessons 4 and 5, the first one is security. Only through Jesus Christ can we ever feel truly secure. He is the only one who can truly meet this need.

The other ingredient is significance. Again, only through Jesus Christ can we ever truly feel significant. As with security, He is the only one who can truly meet our need for significance. The verse for this Lesson, Jeremiah 29:11, says, *"'For I know the plans I have for you,' declares the LORD, 'plans to prosper you and not to harm you, plans to give you hope and a future.'"*

We all need to feel like our lives are making a difference, that each day we live things get better instead of worse. That is why we all need a plan for our lives. Whether you even realize it or not, you do, too. We all do.

> Leading Question: Think about it, just how many things do you do in your life without a plan? (For example: school, college, marriage, where we live, where we go–you do not even go to the grocery store without planning how you will get there and what you will buy, etc.)

But problems occur when the plan for our lives starts to deviate from God's plan. We start thinking we know best. We start believing lies about how to succeed in life and become trapped inside the world's definition of success. We start chasing after pursuits in life that offer everything but produce nothing.

We then start to feel empty inside because we no longer feel significant. But we need to feel significant, which drives us to chase after more pursuits to regain significance. Unfortunately, though, they leave us feeling more of the same. We get stuck on a merry-go-round where we are continually disappointed in life. We get trapped in a vicious cycle of pain and failure.

But thank God He has a better way! He can provide the significance we need. He can provide a purpose for life that includes adequacy, importance and real meaning.

Through His truth, you can step out of your bondage from pursuing inadequate goals that only produce temporary fixes to this problem at best. You can overcome your failure to provide significance in your life by focusing on the truth that you are significant to God.

As we said in Lesson 5, God proved that to us by showing that even when He saw us at our worst, we were still so significant to Him that Jesus died for us. Romans 5:8 says, "*But God demonstrates His own love for us in this: While we were still sinners, Christ died for us.*"

Truth

You are worthwhile to God, the Maker of heaven and earth. As we already said, you are so worthwhile to Him that He died for you, just as you are. Plus, in Genesis 1:26-31 we read, "*Then God said, 'Let Us make man in Our image, according to Our likeness; and let them rule over the fish of the sea and over the birds of the sky and over the cattle and over all the earth, and over every creeping thing that creeps on the earth.' God created man in His own image, in the image of God He created him; male and female He created them. God blessed them; and God said to them, 'Be fruitful and multiply, and fill the earth, and subdue it; and rule over the fish of the sea and over the birds of the sky and over every living thing that moves on the earth.' Then God said, 'Behold, I have given you every plant yielding seed that is on the surface of all the earth, and every tree which has fruit yielding seed; it shall be food for you; and to every beast of the earth and to every bird of the sky and to every thing that moves on the earth which has life, I have given every green plant for food'; and it was so. God saw all that He had made, and behold, it was very good.*"

There is a wealth of information to be gleaned from these verses. Let us summarize what we can learn from them:

1. You are so significant to God that He created you in ***His own image.***
2. You are so significant to God that He has given you dominion over all of His creation on earth (so God wants you to rule over His creation).
3. You are so significant to God that He blessed you.
4. You are so significant to God that He made us male and female so we can continue to reproduce more people who are also formed in His image (we are so significant that God wanted more of us, which means you and me).

5. You are so significant to God that He wants you to be fruitful.
6. You are so significant to God that He wants you to subdue your problems.
7. You are so significant to God that He gave you everything you need to survive.
8. You are so significant to God that He created everything else on earth for you.
9. You are so significant to God that He looked at you after seeing how He created you and said that you are ***very good*** (which is special, considering that after all the other days of creation in Genesis 1, God referred to His creation as "good", and not "very good", as He did here).

Because we are so significant and worthwhile to God, He can be trusted with our future. Psalm 138:8 says, "*The Lord will fulfill His purpose for me...*" As we read in Jeremiah 29:11, God has a particular purpose, a race and a plan for each one of us, including you.

But to fully realize that plan for our life, we need to be willing to get rid of all the unnecessary baggage from the past and our fears of the future that keep us stuck in our emotional wounds. In Hebrews 12:1 we read, "*Therefore, since we are surrounded by such a great cloud of witnesses, let us throw off everything that hinders and the sin that so easily entangles, and let us run with perseverance the race marked out for us.*"

Unless you are willing to honestly deal with your emotional pain and to make healthy, God-approved changes, you will never be able to run your particular race and live the good plan that God has for your life. You will never be able to get your "person" right, so that the whole world will look much better. This is crucial because, as we said before, this race is not a sprint, it is a marathon.

God is giving you a choice. In Deuteronomy 30:15,19 He said, "*See, I set before you today life and prosperity, death and destruction...This day I call heaven and earth as witnesses against you that I have set before you life and death, blessings and curses. Now choose life, so that you and your children may live.*"

Do you want to choose life? Do you want to live God's way so you can have a full life and live under His blessings? Or do you want to continue living your way where you will only experience more of the curse of destruction and disappointment?

Finally we ask you, "Do you want to fully live or do you just want to exist?"

Checking In

Take a minute to review the **Guidelines for Checking In** found in Lesson 1.

Please use this time today to talk about anything you are comfortable with sharing. You can share what has been happening lately in your life or how you feel about what we just discussed. Regardless of the issue, focus on how you feel about it and how it is affecting you.

A good way to get started is by telling the people in your group about how you handled and answered the items from last week's **Acting on the Truth** section. Or maybe you might want to tell them if any of the items were particularly difficult to deal with or hard to understand. You may also tell them if any of the things we just discussed are difficult for you to understand or accept.

At the completion of your time, we would like you to say, "I'm in" signifying that your time is completed. If you do not want to share this week, that is fine. But we still require you to at least say, "I'm in."

To help you get started, you may want to address the following statements and questions:

1. Briefly introduce yourself.
2. Why are you here and what expectations do you have from this ministry?
3. Have you been in a group like this before and what was it like?
4. How do you feel about being here?

Acting on the Truth

1. Do you feel like you are living a life of significance or do you feel like you are just existing (and thus feel empty inside)?

____

____

____

____

2. What have you tried to do to gain the feeling of significance?

____

____

____

____

3. Do you want to start living the life of significance God has for you by following His plan for your life?

____

4. Continue transforming your mind with God's truth by memorizing Jeremiah 29:11, "'*For I know the plans I have for you,' declares the LORD, 'plans to prosper you and not to harm you, plans to give you hope and a future.'*" Each time you say it, spend time thinking about what it means for you and your situation.
5. Continue transforming your mind with God's truth by memorizing John 10:10, "*The thief comes only to steal and kill and destroy; I have come that they may have life, and have it to the full.*" Each time you say it, spend time thinking about what it means for you and your situation.

Transforming Benefits

1. **You can start to really live instead of just existing.** By accepting the truth that you are significant to God and that you matter to Him, you can start the process of living a life of significance and stop merely existing.
2. **Learning to trust God more.** Once you commit to follow the plans He has for your life, you will learn to trust God more. As you follow God and His plans in your life, He will prove He can be trusted in any situation you experience. God will be right beside you each step of the way and He will never leave you to fend for yourself in His plan.
3. **Living one day at a time to keep from feeling overwhelmed.** By choosing to run the race God gives you and follow His plan, you can start living this life one day at a time. We need to live this way because this life is a marathon and not a sprint. It is healthy to focus only on the day ahead of you because you can keep the feeling of being overwhelmed in check. Focusing on the present and not the past or future will help limit the painful feelings of the past and the anxiety and fear of the future.

4. **Continue transforming your mind by dwelling on God's truth.** By memorizing the scripture verses, you will begin filling your mind and heart with God's Truth. You are what you think. Proverbs 23:7 says, "*For as he thinks within himself, so he is*" (NASV). What we think about and dwell on will affect our feelings, which in turn affects our attitudes, which ultimately, affects our behavior. You can begin to transform all of these by spending increasing amounts of time thinking about truth. By memorizing and focusing on the truth in the verses that prove how you can start to live to the fullest, you can change how you think about the status of your life in relation to your painful situation.

Truth 2: Emotional Wounds Can Be Healed

"He heals the brokenhearted and binds up their wounds."
(Psalm 147:3)

Lesson 9

Healing Your Wounds Will Enable You To Find Peace

"Peace I leave with you; My peace I give you.
I do not give to you as the world gives.
Do not let your hearts be troubled and do not be afraid."
(John 14:27)

Why Are You Here?

Leader's Note: As a reminder, please note that next week is Lesson 10. Lesson 10 is where we stop at the end of the lesson and spend the rest of the time having fun. We have historically called Lesson 10 "Game Night" where our members participate in a TV game show we prepared. You can do something similar, or play a board game, or just have a party. We suggest you have snacks and drinks for this lesson and provide prizes for the winners if you play a game (like candy, and make sure there is enough for everyone).

Regardless of what you do next week, we cannot emphasis enough the importance of doing something fun. This has been extremely well received in our groups and almost assuredly your local members will enjoy a week of fun, too. The members from all the Level 2 and 3 small groups should also be invited to join in the fun, so inform your other group leaders about next week, too.

Please read the *Leader's Note* at the end of the **Truth** Section in Lesson 10 for further information on planning for the next lesson.

In Lesson 2 we discussed the **Three Truths About Life:**

1. We all live through painful experiences that can cause emotional wounds (some of which can be hidden).
2. Emotional wounds take longer to heal than physical wounds, but they can still be healed.
3. Jesus Christ wants to heal your emotional wounds.

In Lesson 3 we looked at Truth Number 1 more closely and elaborated on the encouragement that we can find in this truth. As we said:

Regardless of the number or severity of your emotional wounds, you are not alone.

In Lessons 4 through 6, we discussed more encouraging news from this truth when we explained that you are accepted and loved by God and by H.O.P.E. We discussed how acceptance and love are the two factors involved in meeting your need for security, and:

How feeling secure can give you the power to take the first step in adopting a healthy approach to dealing with your pain.

In Lesson 7, we looked at Truth Number 2 more closely and elaborated on the encouragement that we can find in this truth. As we said:

Something can be done about your pain.

In Lesson 7 we also discussed how you need to stop denying your pain, stop playing God and start admitting you are helpless and your situation is beyond your control.

Last week, we showed how you need your emotional wounds healed in order to start living the life of fullness that God intended you to live. We also discussed how God can meet your need to feel significant and worthwhile.

This week, we will continue discussing this encouragement from Truth Number 2 by focusing on another reason why you need your emotional wounds healed:

You need your emotional wounds healed in order for you to find peace.

The word peace can have many different meanings depending on who you ask and the situation they are experiencing. When we are in pain, we often have the tendency to define peace as "the absence of troubles." However, that is not an accurate definition of the word peace. Rather, peace is:

Being calm and at rest on the inside in the midst of (and in spite of) your troubles and pain.

It is not realistic to think we will find inner peace when all our troubles are gone, because as we illustrated in Lesson 7 with the "Whack-A-Mole" game, troubles will continue to keep popping up in our life for as long as we are breathing. There will always be someone or something that tries to take our peace. Even though people and situations will try to take our peace away, the only way they can get our peace is if we give it away. The truth is that we are always in control of it because:

Nobody or nothing can take our peace from us; we must give it away.

Let us illustrate this for you with a message Pastor Joel Osteen preached. There are three methods of flight used by birds: flapping, gliding and soaring. Most birds, like a crow for example, have to flap to fly; their wings have to work for them to stay airborne. A fewer birds, like ducks and geese, can glide for short periods of time. But only a couple birds can soar; these birds can stay airborne without using any flying motion from their wing muscles. Of these birds, only eagles truly know how to soar, with accounts of them being seen as high as 20,000 feet.

The people and situations that have hurt you and caused you pain are like crows to an eagle. Crows will approach an eagle and try to annoy him (take his peace). But in the midst of this turmoil from the crows, eagles will remain calm and not lose their peace. They will simply rise above it, literally. They will catch a thermal and soar to heights a crow cannot reach because a crow cannot soar.

Here is the point of this illustration. God made you to soar. God made you to rise above the pain in your life and enjoy the peace that He alone can bring. But in order to soar, you need to find peace again. In order to find peace, you need your wounds to be healed.

No matter how much pain you are in right now, the sun (and Son) is still shining above the storm clouds. Like an eagle soaring above, you just need a higher perspective to see it, the perspective that only the Lord can provide.

You may be sitting there thinking, "But my peace is long gone. I need to try to get it back, first." Maybe you feel like Job felt when he said, "*I have no peace, no quietness; I have no rest, but only turmoil*" (Job 3:26). Or maybe you feel like Jeremiah did when he said in Lamentations 3:17, "*I have been deprived of peace...*"

If that is you, we want to encourage you that it is possible to regain your peace. Peace is actually one of the benefits of admitting your situation is out of control and turning it over to God's control, as we discussed in Lesson 7. Turning control over to God and following His plan by living it out in your life one day at a time is a sure recipe for peace.

A good example of a situation where an entire nation needed to get its peace back can be found in the book of Exodus. Moses had just led the Israelites out of Egypt and they had reached the Red Sea. The Egyptians changed their mind about letting them go and were bearing down on them.

To the casual observer, it appeared as though the Israelites were trapped. Feeling that way, they lost their peace and became very distressed. But Moses spoke and told them they would soon get their peace back. In Exodus 14:13 Moses said to the people, "*Do not be afraid. Stand firm and you will see the deliverance the LORD will bring you today. The Egyptians you see today you will never see again.*"

After that, God showed His power and parted the waters of the Red Sea. The Israelites went across on dry land, but the water swallowed up the Egyptians as soon as God stopped holding it back.

Just like the Egyptians to the Israelites, the distress and pain you are experiencing today can be left behind forever. The pathway to regaining peace involves trusting in God to heal your wounds. Jeremiah 33:6 says, "*Nevertheless, I will bring health and healing...I will heal My people and will let them enjoy abundant peace.*" In Isaiah 57:19 we read, "'*Peace, peace, to those far and near,' says the LORD. 'And I will heal them.*'" In Romans 15:13 Paul wrote, "*May the God of hope fill you with all joy and peace as you trust in Him...*" Finally, in Isaiah 26:3 we read, "*You will keep in perfect peace him whose mind is steadfast, because he trusts in You.*"

God can be trusted to heal your wounds and give you back your peace so you can soar as He intended. In fact, God cannot produce anything ***but*** peace in one who chooses to trust

Him to heal their pain because it is a part of His very character. In 1 Corinthians 14:33 we read, *"For God is not a God of disorder but of peace."*

He promises to meet our need for peace, too, if we follow His plan and direction. Psalm 85:8 says, *"I will listen to what God the LORD will say; He promises peace to His people..."* He can be trusted to restore peace through His healing; we have His Word on it.

By the way, did you know that researchers have been studying an area in the Red Sea where they believe the crossing by the Israelites happened? (This location is in the Gulf of Aqaba near the beach of Nuweiba, first discovered by Ron Wyatt in 1978. For clarification, there is another potential crossing site near the Strait of Tiran with similar underwater topography marked by coral reefs.) Not surprisingly, some exciting discoveries have been made in this location.

For example, an underwater land bridge has been found at this site (a gently sloping elevated area of land that is several miles wide and only a couple hundred feet below the water's surface that spans from Egypt to Saudi Arabia across a 3,000-5,000 foot deep canal). Computer and physical models have both shown how holding back the water would have exposed this area and allowed all 2-4 million Israelites to cross the sea in only one evening (as we read in Exodus 14:20-24).

Divers in this area have also found the remains of pieces of chariots covered in coral (including chariot wheels, some of which are made of gold, and axels), as well as the coral-encrusted bones of humans and horses. In addition, two Phoenician columns were found, one on either side of this site, that are believed to be a memorial erected by King Solomon to the miraculous Red Sea crossing (as indicated by the inscription still legible on one of the columns).

So as archaeology has once again shown, not only do we have God's Word on it, but we also have His evidence on it, evidence that proves that God has the ability to restore your peace even if He has to "soar" to miraculous heights.

If you have been thinking it would take a miracle for you to overcome your pain and problems and regain your peace, take heart because God is in the business of miracles.

Truth

You can experience peace again. You need your wounds healed to experience peace and soar the way God intended you to soar. It is all a matter of trusting Him to heal your wounds and restore your peace.

It is actually a cycle that feeds back on itself. The more you trust, the more peace you gain. The more peace you have, the more you will trust. ***Now this is one cycle you want to get caught up in!***

Your peace can be found in Jesus Christ and the healing power that only He possesses. Micah 5:5 says, "*And He will be their peace.*" In John 16:33 Jesus said, "*I have told you these things, so that in Me you may have peace. In this world you will have trouble. But take heart! I have overcome the world.*" In Ephesians 2:14 we read, "*For He Himself is our peace...*"

Not only can Jesus heal our emotional wounds, but He also has the power to heal and restore our relationship with God the Father. Romans 5:1 says, "*Therefore, since we have been justified through faith, we have peace with God through our Lord Jesus Christ.*" Colossians 1:20 says, "*...and through Him to reconcile to Himself all things, whether things on earth or things in heaven, by making peace through His blood, shed on the cross.*" Isaiah 53:5 reads, "*But He was pierced for our transgressions, He was crushed for our iniquities; the punishment that brought us peace was upon Him, and by His wounds we are healed.*"

Since Jesus can be trusted to restore our peace with God the Father through the cross, He can certainly be trusted to restore our peace in the midst of our suffering and pain, too, through the wholeness and healing that only He can provide. But in order for this to happen, you have to choose to trust Christ and His plan for healing your pain. It is a choice that we are encouraged to make in Romans 14:19 where Paul wrote, "*Let us therefore make every effort to do what leads to peace...*" In Philippians 4:9 Paul also wrote, "*Whatever you have learned or received or heard from me, or seen in me–put it into practice. And the God of peace will be with you.*"

No matter how bad you feel today, God can be trusted to heal your pain and restore peace in your world. You ***can*** reach the point in your life where you can experience what David felt when he wrote, "*I will lie down and sleep in peace, for you alone, O LORD, make me dwell in safety*" (Psalm 4:8).

And you can arrive at the place where you can enjoy the benefits of living in peace. Benefits like that described in Proverbs 14:30, "*A heart at peace gives life to the body...*" Or like that described in Philippians 4:6,7, "*Do not be anxious about anything, but in everything, by prayer and petition, with thanksgiving, present your requests to God. And the peace of God, which transcends all understanding, will guard your hearts and your minds in Christ Jesus.*" Or finally, like we read in Job 22:21, "*Submit to God and be at peace with Him; in this way prosperity will come to you.*"

Checking In

Take a minute to review the **Guidelines for Checking In** found in Lesson 1.

Please use this time today to talk about anything you are comfortable with sharing. You can share what has been happening lately in your life or how you feel about what we just discussed. Regardless of the issue, focus on how you feel about it and how it is affecting you.

A good way to get started is by telling the people in your group about how you handled and answered the items from last week's **Acting on the Truth** section. Or maybe you might want to tell them if any of the items were particularly difficult to deal with or hard to understand. You may also tell them if any of the things we just discussed are difficult for you to understand or accept.

At the completion of your time, we would like you to say, "I'm in" signifying that your time is completed. If you do not want to share this week, that is fine. But we still require you to at least say, "I'm in."

To help you get started, you may want to address the following statements and questions:

1. Briefly introduce yourself.
2. Why are you here and what expectations do you have from this ministry?
3. Have you been in a group like this before and what was it like?
4. How do you feel about being here?

Acting on the Truth

1. What is your level of peace today?

2. Do you want to try to regain your peace?

3. Are you willing to trust God and follow His plan for healing your pain and restoring your peace?

4. Do you want to soar the way God intended for you?

5. Have you ever accepted the healing restoration of your relationship with God in your life offered through Jesus Christ? If not, would you like to? If so, turn to the **Acting on the Truth** section of Lesson 12 and read numbers 2, 3 and 4 which will help you work through this decision.

6. Continue transforming your mind with God's truth by memorizing John 16:33 where Jesus said, "*I have told you these things, so that in Me you may have peace. In this world you will have trouble. But take heart! I have overcome the world.*" Each time you say it, spend time thinking about what it means for you and your situation.
7. Continue transforming your mind with God's truth by memorizing 1 Corinthians 14:33, "*For God is not a God of disorder but of peace.*" Each time you say it, spend time thinking about what it means for you and your situation.
8. Continue transforming your mind with God's truth by memorizing Romans 15:13, "*May the God of hope fill you with all joy and peace as you trust in Him...*" Each time you say it, spend time thinking about what it means for you and your situation.

Transforming Benefits

1. **Trusting God for His healing brings peace.** As we read in Isaiah 26:3, "*You will keep in perfect peace him whose mind is steadfast, because he trusts in You.*" By trusting in God and His ability to bring wholeness and healing into your life, you can experience peace again.
2. **Peace improves your physical health, too.** Proverbs 14:30 says, "*A heart at peace gives life to the body...*" Therefore, the benefits of trusting God and His plan for healing will not only improve your emotional health, but also your physical health as a bonus of living in peace.
3. **Peace is a powerful spiritual and emotional weapon.** Maintaining your peace in the midst of your troubles will help you to say "No" to temptations. It will help you develop a greater level of trust, which in turn will help you avoid your old pattern of behavior during difficult times.
4. **Continue transforming your mind by dwelling on God's truth.** By memorizing the scripture verses, you will begin filling your mind and heart with God's Truth. You are what you think. Proverbs 23:7 says, "*For as he thinks within himself, so he is*" (NASV). What we think about and dwell on will affect our feelings, which in turn affects our attitudes, which ultimately, affects our behavior. You can begin to transform all of these by spending increasing amounts of time thinking about truth. By memorizing and focusing on the truth in the verses that show how to start enjoying a life of peace, you can change how you think about the status of your life in relation to your painful situation.

Truth 2: Emotional Wounds Can Be Healed

"He heals the brokenhearted and binds up their wounds."
(Psalm 147:3)

Lesson 10

Healing Your Wounds Will Enable You To Find Joy and Happiness

"You have made known to me the path of life;
You will fill me with joy in Your presence,
with eternal pleasures at Your right hand."
(Psalm 16:11)

Why Are You Here?

In Lesson 2 we discussed the **Three Truths About Life:**

1. We all live through painful experiences that can cause emotional wounds (some of which can be hidden).
2. Emotional wounds take longer to heal than physical wounds, but they can still be healed.
3. Jesus Christ wants to heal your emotional wounds.

In Lesson 3 we looked at Truth Number 1 more closely and elaborated on the encouragement that we can find in this truth. As we said:

Regardless of the number or severity of your emotional wounds, you are not alone.

In Lessons 4 through 6, we discussed more encouraging news from this truth when we explained that you are accepted and loved by God and by H.O.P.E. We discussed how acceptance and love are the two factors involved in meeting your need for security, and:

How feeling secure can give you the power to take the first step in adopting a healthy approach to dealing with your pain.

In Lesson 7 we looked at Truth Number 2 more closely and elaborated on the encouragement that we can find in this truth. As we said:

Something can be done about your pain.

In Lesson 7 we also discussed how you need to stop denying your pain, stop playing God and start admitting you are helpless and your situation is beyond your control.

In Lesson 8, we showed how you need your emotional wounds healed in order to start living the life of fullness that God intended for you to live. We also discussed how God can meet your need to feel significant and worthwhile.

Last week we showed how you need your emotional wounds healed in order for you to find peace.

This week, we will continue discussing this encouragement from Truth Number 2 by focusing on another reason why you need your emotional wounds healed:

You need your emotional wounds healed in order to find joy and happiness.

Happiness has become a hot topic for psychology today. There have been numerous studies done in the area and we would like to summarize a few of the findings:

1. Lottery winners go back to their previous level of happiness within three months of receiving their money.
2. Getting more "stuff" does not bring happiness.

3. Once your basic needs are met, money has little to no effect on happiness (a comparison between the rich and poor showed no difference in their level of happiness).
4. Happy people have better health, are more productive, make more money, are more charitable and are more creative.

Leading Question: Do any of these findings surprise you?

The main point we want to make, though, is that in essence:

Psychologists have learned that people are not good predictors of what will make them happy.

That is because the things that bring us pleasure are always changing and always escalating. We always want what is bigger and better.

Yet, we all seek joy and happiness, and we always will. God designed us that way. He designed the world to be full of pleasures for us. So why would He not want us to enjoy them?

The problem is that we have misunderstood what the words pleasure, happiness and joy really mean. So let's look at these three words more closely.

1. **Pleasure:** Pleasure is found in what you do. It is temporary and external. It is the pursuit of your own will and it is sustained only as long as the circumstances are right. It will always leave you empty. In 1 Timothy 5:6, Paul addressed the emptiness of pleasure when writing about widows he said, "*The widow who lives for pleasure is dead even while she lives.*"

   King Solomon, arguably the richest man who ever lived, spent the first part of his life searching for pleasure. His conclusion of all his efforts to find pleasure can be found in Ecclesiastes 2:11, "*But as I looked at everything I had worked so hard to accomplish, it was all so meaningless. It was like chasing the wind. There was nothing really worthwhile anywhere*" (NLT).

2. **Happiness:** Happiness is found in who you are. It is internal and results from your choice of character. It lasts as long as you do not compromise your character; it is sustained as long as your character is right. It is not dependent on circumstances and can be maintained in spite of circumstances as along as you maintain your integrity.

Happiness is an inside job. Psalm 119:1 says, *"Happy are people of integrity..."* (NLT). In Proverbs 16:20 we read, *"...those who trust the LORD will be happy"* (NLT). Psalm 146:5 says, *"But happy are those who have the God of Israel as their helper, whose hope is in the LORD their God"* (NLT).

3. **Joy:** Joy is found in Jesus Christ. Joy is internal and eternal. It is sustained by Jesus Christ and is unrelated to circumstances. It cannot be taken away. It is the realization of how much God loves you and how much you mean to Him. It happens as you pursue God's will for your life.

   Joy is also an inside job. In John 15:11 Jesus said, *"These things I have spoken to you so that My joy may be in you, and that your joy may be made full"* (NASV). Again in John 17:13 Jesus said, *"But now I come to You; and these things I speak in the world so that they may have My joy made full in themselves"* (NASV).

Let us summarize these points:

You can be happy and full of joy when bad things are occurring around you if good things are happening inside you.

Truth

To begin the process of creating a life where good things are happening inside you, you first need your emotional wounds healed. You need to break the connection between:

- Temporary pleasure and lasting happiness.
- What you do and who you are.
- Your circumstances and your character.

God wants you to find happiness and joy again. ***And you can!*** God wants you live the way He described in Isaiah 55:12, *"For you will go out in joy and be led forth in peace; the mountains and hills will burst into song before you, and all the trees of the field will clap their hands"* (NASV).

God does not want us to settle for what we think will provide us joy and happiness. We think we know best, but our choices are fleeting. When we chase after our own desires, we live as a child who settles for mud pies down in a swamp when God offers us the most elaborate banquet feast ever at the most beautiful palace imaginable.

Plus, as we already said, we are not good predictors of what will make us happy.

This is directly applicable to what we think is the best way to handle our troubles and emotional pain. But to reiterate, on our own, we do not know the best way to deal with our situation.

Fortunately, though, God does. This ministry is full of people who can testify to that, people who have followed His plan for dealing with their pain, people who can encourage you to heed what Christ has taught them in this regard. As we read in Proverbs 3:13, "*Happy is the person who finds wisdom and gains understanding*" (NLT).

All you need to do is ask God for His help in overcoming your pain and He has promised that He will help you. In John 16:24 Jesus said, "*Until now you have not asked for anything in My Name. Ask and you will receive, and your joy will be complete.*"

Not only does God want you to find happiness and joy again, but so do we. We want you to be happy again and to experience the joy of the Lord. We want you to get up every morning and be able to say, "*This is the day the LORD has made; let us rejoice and be glad in it*" (Psalm 118:24).

We want you to laugh and have fun again.

And we are going to start on that right now.

> Leader's Note: At this point, we stop the lesson and spend the rest of the time this week having fun. We have a long history of having what we call "Game Night" where our members participate in a TV game show we prepared. You can do something similar, or play a board game, or just have a party. We suggest you have snacks and drinks for this lesson and provide prizes for the winners if you play a game (like candy, and make sure there is enough for everyone).
>
> The members from all the Level 2 and 3 small groups should also be invited to join your group so everyone in H.O.P.E. can take a break from the hard part of their journey and just have fun. For the Level 2 and 3 groups, we encourage the leaders to only do either the lesson or **Checking In** this week in their groups so they can all finish at approximately the same time and join the fun with your Level 1 group.

Regardless of what you do this week, we cannot emphasis enough the importance of doing something fun. This has been extremely well received in our groups and almost assuredly your local members will enjoy a week of fun, too.

There is no scheduled **Checking In** for this lesson in the *Doorway to H.O.P.E.* group. However, if someone really wants or needs to do so, we encourage you to make arrangements for them to check in after the fun.

Acting on the Truth

1. What is your level of happiness today?

    ____

    ____

    ____

    ____

2. Do you want to try to regain your happiness?

    ____

3. Are you willing to trust God and follow His plan for healing your pain and restoring your happiness and joy?

    ____

4. Do you want to experience true, everlasting joy that can only be found in Jesus Christ?

    ____

5. Continue transforming your mind with God's truth by memorizing Psalm 16:11, "*You have made known to me the path of life; You will fill me with joy in Your presence, with eternal pleasures at Your right hand.*" Each time you say it, spend time thinking about what it means for you and your situation.
6. Continue transforming your mind with God's truth by memorizing Proverbs 16:20, "*...those who trust the LORD will be happy*" (NLT). Each time you say it, spend time thinking about what it means for you and your situation.
7. Continue transforming your mind with God's truth by memorizing John 15:11, "*These things I have spoken to you so that My joy may be in you, and that your joy may*

be made full" (NASV). Each time you say it, spend time thinking about what it means for you and your situation.

Transforming Benefits

1. **Trusting God for His healing brings happiness.** As we read in Proverbs 16:20, "... *those who trust the LORD will be happy*" (NLT). By trusting in God and His ability to bring wholeness and healing into your life, you can experience happiness again. Happiness can be developed and maintained in spite of your pain and circumstances if you trust in the Lord to help you through it.
2. **There are genuine benefits of happiness.** As we discussed, some of the many benefits of being happy include: better health, more productivity, more charitability and more creativity. So as you can see, regaining your happiness can bring many healthy improvements in your life.
3. **The joy of the Lord is an inside job.** Real, everlasting joy can only be found in Jesus Christ. Your joy can only be made full in Him. Joy is not dependent on circumstances, so it can be restored in the midst of your pain. When you allow good things to happen inside you (the transformation that comes from Jesus), you can experience true joy.
4. **Continue transforming your mind by dwelling on God's truth.** By memorizing the scripture verses, you will begin filling your mind and heart with God's Truth. You are what you think. Proverbs 23:7 says, "*For as he thinks within himself, so he is*" (NASV). What we think about and dwell on will affect our feelings, which in turn affects our attitudes, which ultimately, affects our behavior. You can begin to transform all of these by spending increasing amounts of time thinking about truth. By memorizing and focusing on the truth in the verses that show how to start enjoying a life of happiness and joy, you can change how you think about your status in life in relation to your painful situation.

Truth 3: Jesus Wants to Heal Your Emotional Wounds

"'I will restore you to health and heal your wounds,' declares the LORD..."
(Jeremiah 30:17)

Lesson 11

Jesus Is Your Doorway To Wholeness And Healing

"But He was pierced for our transgressions,
He was crushed for our iniquities;
the punishment that brought us peace was upon Him,
and by His wounds we are healed."
(Isaiah 53:5)

Why Are You Here?

In Lesson 2 we discussed the **Three Truths About Life:**

1. We all live through painful experiences that can cause emotional wounds (some of which can be hidden).
2. Emotional wounds take longer to heal than physical wounds, but they can still be healed.
3. Jesus Christ wants to heal your emotional wounds.

In Lesson 3 we looked at Truth Number 1 more closely and elaborated on the encouragement that we can find in this truth. As we said:

> ***Regardless of the number or severity of your emotional wounds, you are <u>not</u> <u>alone</u>.***

In Lessons 4 through 6, we discussed more encouraging news from this truth when we explained that you are accepted and loved by God and by H.O.P.E. We discussed how acceptance and love are the two factors involved in meeting your need for security, and:

> ***How feeling secure can give you the power to take the first step in adopting a healthy approach to dealing with your pain.***

In Lesson 7 we looked at Truth Number 2 more closely and elaborated on the encouragement that we can find in this truth. As we said:

> ***Something <u>can</u> be done about your pain.***

In Lesson 7 we also discussed how you need to stop denying your pain, stop playing God and start admitting you are helpless and your situation is beyond your control.

In Lesson 8, we showed how you need your emotional wounds healed in order to start living the life of fullness that God intended for you to live. We also discussed how God can meet your need to feel significant and worthwhile.

In Lesson 9 we showed how you need your emotional wounds healed in order for you to find peace.

Last week, we showed how you need your emotional wounds healed in order for you to find joy and happiness.

This week, we will focus on the final truth, Truth Number 3, which says that Jesus Christ wants to heal your emotional wounds. The encouragement we want to share with you today is:

> ***There is someone who actually <u>wants</u> to help and do something about your pain.***

Jesus wants to help you overcome your hurt and pain. It does not matter where you have been, what you have been through or what you have done. He still wants to help you. As we read in Isaiah 57:18, *"I have seen his ways, but I will heal him; I will guide him and restore comfort to him..."*

Jesus wants to do this because you are worthwhile to Him (a concept we will expand upon in the *Names of H.O.P.E.* Level 2 small groups). As we have already discussed in Truths 1 and 2, feeling worthwhile comes from feeling secure and significant. These two feelings can only be truly satisfied in Jesus Christ.

Not only does Jesus want to help you, but realistically He is the only one who can do something about your pain. He is the only one who can actually transform you and help you overcome it in a way that will bring about lasting and eternal change in your life. He is the only one who has all the necessary credentials to get the job done.

As we discussed last week, it is an inside job. Without making the necessary changes on the inside, all other attempts to take care of your hurt and pain will only bring fleeting, temporary fixes at best. It will never last until you allow God to work on you from the inside out.

In addition to feeling secure and significant, another fundamental need we all have is to change and grow. This leads to the principle that:

> ***If you are not changing, then you are not growing. If you are not growing, then you are not really living because the two are directly related.***

> Leading Question: How are you feeling today? Do you feel like you are changing, growing and really living, or not? Are you ready to start or are you ready to experience more of it?

Growth always means change, healthy change. Just as with security and significance, Jesus is the only one who can meet the need in us to change because:

> ***Exposure to Jesus Christ always brings change.***

Jesus Christ is all about changed lives.

Let us illustrate this concept for you by comparing a few possible situations with the relative verses that speak to how He can bring change.

Look at the following scenarios:

If you:	**Jesus brings change by:**
1. Have been abandoned or rejected,	1. Promising to never reject us. "*Though my father and mother forsake me, the LORD will receive me*" (Psalm 27:10). "*Never will I leave you; never will I forsake you*" (Hebrews 13:5).
2. Have been disowned by your own family,	2. Offering to be your new family. "... *you have received a spirit of adoption as sons by which we cry out, 'Abba! Father!'*" (Romans 8:15, NASV).
3. Are feeling alienated,	3. Giving us citizenship. "...*you are no longer strangers and aliens, but you are fellow citizens, with the saints, and are of God's household*" (Eph. 2:19, NASV).
4. Are feeling brokenhearted,	4. Restoring broken hearts. "*The LORD is close to the brokenhearted and saves those who are crushed in spirit*" (Psalm 34:18).
5. Are feeling trapped in your troubles,	5. Delivering us from our troubles. "*Many are the afflictions of the righteous, but the LORD delivers him out of them all*" (Psalm 34:19, NASV) and He will "...*proclaim liberty to captives...*" (Isaiah 61:1, NASV).
6. Are feeling unloved,	6. Being the very essence of love that never ends. "...*God is love*" (1 John 4:8) and "... *His love endures forever*" (Psalm 136:6).
7. Are feeling distressed or anxious,	7. Being our peace. "*For He Himself is our peace...*" (Ephesians 2:14).
8. Are mourning and in despair,	8. Promising to "...*comfort all who mourn, to grant those who mourn in Zion, giving them a garland instead of ashes, the oil of gladness instead of mourning...*" (Isaiah 61:2,3, NASV).

Get the picture?

The truth is, for whatever situation you find yourself in today, God can grant you a way to change and overcome your situation. This way is one that will not only change you, but a way that will also transform the very nature of who you are. This way, the only way, is in and through Jesus Christ. As Jesus said in John 14:6, *"I am the way and the truth and the life. No one comes to the Father except through Me."*

Hopefully you have already started to change while you have been in this group. But there is so much more change God has planned for you, positive, healthy, life transforming change, which means that you now have to decide if you want to allow God to make these changes in your life.

> Leading Question: Let us ask again, "How are you feeling today?" Are you ready for a change?

Truth

Jesus is ready, willing and able to help you regain emotional wholeness and healing. He is standing there with His arms open wide waiting to receive you. He is not interested in just fine-tuning you, like so many of the other things you may have already tried. Instead, He wants to change you eternally by transforming your very nature.

It is here that you need to recognize that this process is a journey; it is a marathon and not a sprint, which happens one day at a time. God's economy of time is very different than ours. So you need to fix your eyes on the final destination, emotional and spiritual wholeness, and commit yourself to working toward that.

This is not a time to give up or fall back into your old habits of dealing with your pain. This is the time to harness the momentum you have already developed and press on toward the prize. As Paul said in Philippians 3:13,14, *"Brethren, I do not regard myself as having laid hold of it yet; but one thing I do: forgetting what lies behind and reaching forward to what lies ahead, I press on toward the goal for the prize of the upward call of God in Christ Jesus"* (NASV).

So next week, we will discuss the opportunity we have for you to allow God to make changes in you that will lead to a transformed life.

Leader's Note: After completing this lesson and prior to Lesson 12, it is highly recommended that all the leaders of this group meet to discuss the small groups for Level 2. To aid in this discussion and planning, we have provided a **Checklist for Entry into a Level 2 *Names of H.O.P.E.* Small Group** in **Appendix C**. This checklist is intended to be used to help determine which members are ready to move on to a Level 2 group.

In addition, we highly recommend that you read through the **Acting on the Truth** section for Lesson 12 prior to the next meeting. This will help you with the process of formally setting your small groups for Level 2. Your group leaders should determine which members should be placed into which small groups and who will be the leaders of each small group. In most Level 1 groups, the makeup of small groups (and their leaders) becomes evident during the course of this level. But it is still wise to set the small groups prior to meeting for the final lesson. This creates a smooth transition into Level 2.

You should also determine where each small group will meet starting next week (making sure that you have the meeting space available). Plus, if you have not already done so, it is a good idea to decide how the ordering of Level 2 books will be handled.

We also recommend that at this point you make it clear to your Level 1 group members that you will be creating small groups at the end of Lesson 12 and that you will do all you can to keep those members together who have become comfortable with one another. Also, inform those who have recently joined the group and are not yet ready for Level 2 that you will be repeating Level 1 and they are welcome to join that group again. If you know when Level 1 will begin meeting again, inform them of that, too.

We have learned that it is best to keep your group members informed of what to expect next and minimize the surprises for group members.

Checking In

Take a minute to review the **Guidelines for Checking In** found in Lesson 1.

Please use this time today to talk about anything you are comfortable with sharing. You can share what has been happening lately in your life or how you feel about what we just discussed. Regardless of the issue, focus on how you feel about it and how it is affecting you.

A good way to get started is by telling the people in your group about how you handled and answered the items from last week's **Acting on the Truth** section. Or maybe you might want to tell them if any of the items were particularly difficult to deal with or hard to understand. You may also tell them if any of the things we just discussed are difficult for you to understand or accept. We also encourage you to look at and comment on how you feel about number 1 in this week's **Acting on the Truth** section (which refers to advancing to Level 2).

At the completion of your time, we would like you to say, "I'm in" signifying that your time is completed. If you do not want to share this week, that is fine. But we still require you to at least say, "I'm in."

To help you get started, you may want to address the following statements and questions:

1. Briefly introduce yourself.
2. Why are you here and what expectations do you have from this ministry?
3. Have you been in a group like this before and what was it like?
4. How do you feel about being here?

Acting on the Truth

1. This week, commit yourself to pray about taking the next step. Next week in the last lesson of the program, we will give you an opportunity to take the next step as we create new Level 2 *Names of H.O.P.E.* small groups.
2. Continue transforming your mind with God's truth by memorizing Isaiah 57:18, "*I have seen his ways, but I will heal him; I will guide him and restore comfort to him...*" Each time you say it, spend time thinking about what it means for you and your situation.
3. Continue transforming your mind with God's truth by memorizing Hebrews 13:5, "*Never will I leave you; never will I forsake you.*" Each time you say it, spend time thinking about what it means for you and your situation.
4. Continue transforming your mind with God's truth by memorizing Psalm 34:19, "*Many are the afflictions of the righteous, but the LORD delivers him out of them all*"

(NASV). Each time you say it, spend time thinking about what it means for you and your situation.

5. Continue transforming your mind with God's truth by memorizing Psalm 34:18, *"The LORD is close to the brokenhearted and saves those who are crushed in spirit."* Each time you say it, spend time thinking about what it means for you and your situation.
6. Continue transforming your mind with God's truth by memorizing Philippians 3:13,14, *"Brethren, I do not regard myself as having laid hold of it yet; but one thing I do: forgetting what lies behind and reaching forward to what lies ahead, I press on toward the goal for the prize of the upward call of God in Christ Jesus"* (NASV). Each time you say it, spend time thinking about what it means for you and your situation.

Transforming Benefits

1. **Living a transformed life characterized by spiritual and emotional wholeness.** If you take the next step and stick to it, you can reap the benefits of living a life of spiritual and emotional wholeness. In addition, God promises to restore you and your situation when He says in Joel 2:25, *"Then I will make up to you for the years that the swarming locust has eaten..."* (NASV). If you do, you will not regret it.
2. **Continue transforming your mind by dwelling on God's truth.** By memorizing the scripture verses, you will begin filling your mind and heart with God's Truth. You are what you think. Proverbs 23:7 says, *"For as he thinks within himself, so he is"* (NASV). What we think about and dwell on will affect our feelings, which in turn affects our attitudes, which ultimately, affects our behavior. You can begin to transform all of these by spending increasing amounts of time thinking about truth. By memorizing and focusing on the truth in the verses that prove how you can experience wholeness and healing through Jesus Christ and His process of transformation, you can change how you think about your status in life in relation to your painful situation.

Truth 3: Jesus Wants to Heal Your Emotional Wounds

"'I will restore you to health and heal your wounds,' declares the LORD..."
(Jeremiah 30:17)

Lesson 12

Walking Through The Doorway To Wholeness And Healing

"So I say to you: Ask and it will be given to you;
seek and you will find; knock and the door will be opened to you.
For everyone who asks receives; he who seeks finds;
and to him who knocks, the door will be opened."
(Luke 11:9,10)

Why Are You Here?

For the past 11 lessons, we have been focused on the **Three Truths About Life:**

1. We all live through painful experiences that can cause emotional wounds (some of which can be hidden).
2. Emotional wounds take longer to heal than physical wounds, but they can still be healed.
3. Jesus Christ wants to heal your emotional wounds.

To recap, in Lesson 3 we looked at Truth Number 1 more closely and elaborated on the encouragement that we can find in this truth. As we said:

Regardless of the number or severity of your emotional wounds, you are not alone.

In Lessons 4 through 6, we discussed more encouraging news from this truth when we explained that you are accepted and loved by God and by H.O.P.E. We discussed how acceptance and love are the two factors involved in meeting your need for security, and:

How feeling secure can give you the power to take the first step in adopting a healthy approach to dealing with your pain.

In Lesson 7 we looked at Truth Number 2 more closely and elaborated on the encouragement that we can find in this truth. As we said:

Something can be done about your pain.

In Lesson 7 we also discussed how you need to stop denying your pain, stop playing God and start admitting you are helpless and your situation is beyond your control.

In Lesson 8, we showed how you need your emotional wounds healed in order to start living the life of fullness that God intended for you to live. We also discussed how God can meet your need to feel significant and worthwhile.

In Lesson 9 we showed how you need your emotional wounds healed in order for you to find peace.

In Lesson 10 we showed how you need your emotional wounds healed in order for you to find joy and happiness.

Last week we focused on the final truth, Truth Number 3, which says that Jesus Christ wants to heal your emotional wounds. The encouragement we shared from that truth was that:

There is someone who actually wants to help and do something about your pain.

Jesus wants to help you overcome your hurt and pain. He is standing there with His arms open wide just waiting for you to come to Him. In the verse for this lesson, Jesus said, "*So I say to you: Ask and it will be given to you; seek and you will find; knock and the door will be opened to you. For everyone who asks receives; he who seeks finds; and to him who knocks, the door will be opened*" (Luke 11:9,10).

Jesus is your Doorway to wholeness and healing, but He is also the perfect gentleman. He will not force His way upon you; you have to decide for yourself and choose to come to Him. As we just read, if you knock, He will open the door so you can walk on in. But the key is:

You have to knock.

There are three points that need to be discussed at this time.

1. There is a saying, "Pain and suffering will color your whole world." This is a true statement. But there is another true statement that needs to be added to this one that is even more important. Pain and suffering will color your whole world, but:

   You get to choose the color.

2. Another critically important truth that must be remembered is:

   There are no hopeless situations, only people who have grown hopeless about their situation.

   Things are never hopeless because God is always willing to help if you will only turn to Him and seek His help. It does not matter how hopeless you may have become about your situation, either. It also does not matter how bad things appear right now, what you have done, what has been done to you, where you have been or what you have experienced.

   If you are in a hole, Jesus is ready, willing and able to help you out. And it does not matter if the hole you are in was dug by you or someone else; His offer still stands. That is what God's grace is all about. He wants to help you overcome your pain and live the victorious life He intended you to life.

3. Even more important than how Jesus wants to help you overcome your pain and live the victorious life He intended you to life here on earth:

   Through His grace, Jesus also wants you to live an eternal life with Him in heaven.

If you have yet to experience God's saving grace in your life, you must understand that this is yet another need you have. In fact, it is the most important need you will ever have. You need to be saved from the guilt and power of sin in your life, and the only way to do that is by accepting the one and only Savior, Jesus Christ.

We all have the need for a Savior because sin has separated us from a holy and perfect God. Yet perfection is what Jesus said is required to approach God when He said, "*Be perfect, therefore, as your heavenly Father is perfect*" (Matthew 5:48). However, none of us are perfect, as we read in Romans 3:23, "*...for all have sinned and fall short of the glory of God...*"

The sin in our lives also means that we deserve punishment, which we read about in Romans 6:23 where it says, "*For the wages of sin is death...*" And the meaning of this verse can be found in Revelation 20:15 where it says, "*If anyone's name was not found written in the book of life, he was thrown into the lake of fire.*" Revelation 20:10 describes what will happen there when it says, "*They will be tormented day and night for ever and ever.*"

We deserve punishment, but as we have already discussed in previous lessons, God loves us so much that He does not want to punish us. Therefore, in His love He provided us a way to be saved from the penalty of our sins, the one and only way, through His Son Jesus Christ. Jesus made that clear when He said, "*I am the way and the truth and the life. No one comes to the Father except through Me*" (John 14:6).

Jesus, being perfect and sinless, suffered and died a substitutionary death on our behalf that satisfied God's judgment on all our sin. He then rose again from the grave in victory over sin and death in order to purchase a place in heaven for us.

He paid the full price when He died on the cross and enabled us to go free from the penalty we deserved for the sin in our lives. Hebrews 9:15 says, "*For Christ died to set them free from the penalty of the sins they had committed...*" (NLT). In Christ, "*... we have redemption through His blood, the forgiveness of sins, in accordance with the riches of God's grace...*" (Ephesians 1:7) because, "*God presented Him as a sacrifice of atonement, through faith in His blood*" (Romans 3:25).

Since Jesus Christ has already paid the penalty for our sins, He can now offer heaven to us as a free gift. Romans 6:23 continues on to say, "*...but the free gift of God is eternal life in Christ Jesus our Lord*" (NASV). Since it is free, there is nothing we can do to earn it or deserve it. There is no amount of good deeds or penance or anything else that can get you into heaven.

Even though heaven is a free gift, we all still share some responsibility in taking advantage of this free offer. As we already said, Jesus is a perfect gentleman and He will not force His way in. You have to choose to accept His offer.

The way you accept it is by faith, which is a ***transfer of your trust*** from what you thought would get you into heaven to Jesus Christ alone and His finished work on the cross. Ephesians 2:8,9 says, *"For it is by grace you have been saved, through faith–and this not from yourselves, it is the gift of God–not by works, so that no one can boast."*

You mean so much to God and He loves you so much that Jesus died for you to save you for all of eternity. Not only that, He did it when he saw you at your worst. As it says in Romans 5:8, *"But God demonstrates His own love for us in this: While we were still sinners, Christ died for us."* So no matter how you feel today and how you feel about how you have been living, the offer still stands.

You have now come to the point in your journey toward wholeness and healing where, as they say, "The rubber meets the road." Just as when you started this group, you have come to a point where you have another decision to make. If you have never accepted God's free gift of eternal life, then you actually have two decisions to make:

1. You have to decide whether or not you are going to take the next step and surrender to God's will and His plan to help you overcome your painful experiences.
2. You have to decide if you want to accept Jesus as your Savior and ask Him to come into your life and begin a relationship with you.

These two steps go hand in hand. If you choose neither, or just one without the other, you will never live the life God intended you to live. Plus, if you do not choose the second, the Bible says you will not live an eternal life in heaven, either.

But if you choose to take both steps, you will not regret it. We can guarantee it. But that does not mean much compared to the fact that God guarantees it; we have His Word on it. If this still seems like a scary proposition to you, take heart in the fact that you will not have to do it alone. We will be there with you every step of the way, and more importantly God will, too.

So let us ask, "Are you ready to knock?"

Truth

God gave His Son Jesus Christ for you. If He gave you the ultimate gift, would He withhold anything else? No, He will not! Romans 8:32 says, "*He who did not spare His own Son, but delivered Him over for us all, how will He not also with Him freely give us all things?*" (NASV). He wants to give you the life of victory, joy, peace and fullness that He always intended you to live.

Hopefully you would agree that this program contains some good lessons for those who are hurting and are in need. But even the greatest lessons in the world will do no good unless they are acted upon. So you have now come to the place where you need to act on these lessons. You have come to the point where you need to make your decision about whether or not you want to allow God to transform your life. If you have not already done so, you also need to decide if you want to accept God's free offer of eternal life through His Son, Jesus Christ.

The Bible says that we can know right now that we have eternal life if we accept Jesus. In 1 John 5:13 it says, "*I write these things to you who believe in the Name of the Son of God so that you may know that you have eternal life.*" So even if you have already taken that step, let these words bring you comfort and assurance today.

If you are afraid of taking either of these steps, be assured that God will be there every step of the way for you and so will H.O.P.E. If you commit to taking this journey, we will commit to helping you through it.

Jesus is your Doorway to H.O.P.E. and we will help you walk through that door. To that end, let us ask you two final questions, "Aren't you tired of trying to carry all your pain alone? Won't you open the Door and take the next step and let Jesus come into your life and help you?"

> <u>Leader's Note:</u> Assuming that your group leaders have already met to discuss Level 2 small groups (as recommended in the <u>*Leader's Note*</u> at the end of Lesson 11), at this point we recommend that you formally set all small groups prior to **Checking In**. To do that, go through the **Acting on the Truth** section in the group this week. As you do, give your group members all the information they will need to transition into Level 2, including who their leaders will be, where they will meet and who will be ordering the Level 2 books.

For those who are not yet ready for Level 2, inform them of what to expect next, too, including when and where you will begin the next Level 1 group. If there are any members who have attended all (or most) of Level 1 that your group leaders have decided should not yet move on to Level 2, we recommend that you take them aside and inform them of why you have made this decision. At that point, encourage them to attend the next Level 1 session and share with them how they can ready themselves to move into Level 2 when the next time arrives.

Acting on the Truth

1. This week we will do this section in the group prior to **Checking In** because we have a plan in place for you to be able to take your next steps, and we want to address this plan now.
2. The first part of this plan includes asking the question, "Have you come to the place where you have accepted God's free gift of eternal life through Jesus Christ?" Next we want to ask, "If you have not, what is keeping you from doing so?" Finally, let us ask, if you have not, "Are you ready to do so now?"

___

3. If you are ready to do this, please pray and ask Him to come into your life, forgive your sins and be your Savior. If you want, we will be happy to do that with you right now before we move on. Are you willing to do so now? If you are not comfortable with doing this now, we can do it after the group or you can do it on your own. It is important to remember that there are no magic words here; it is a matter of your heart. Romans 10:13 says, "*Everyone who calls on the Name of the Lord will be saved*", so we have assurance that He will hear us and come into our hearts and have a real relationship with us. John 3:16 also says, "*For God so loved the world that He gave His one and only Son, that whoever believes in Him shall not perish but have eternal life.*"
4. If you have just accepted Christ, or if you have done it previously, read and memorize John 6:47, "*Truly, truly, I say to you, he who believes has eternal life*" (NASV). As with any friend, you grow a relationship by spending time with them. Do so with Jesus this week by spending time praying and talking to Him and stopping to listen to Him. Also, please record the date here. You can look back on this date for the rest of your life as your "Spiritual Birthday."

___

5. The second part of this plan includes becoming a member of one of our *Names of H.O.P.E.* Level 2 small groups. At the end of this lesson you will find two copies of the **Contract for Membership in *Names of H.O.P.E.*** If you are ready to join one of these groups, please fill out one copy of this contract and return it to us. Then fill out the other copy and keep it for yourself in a place where you will see it often as a reminder of your commitment to your new group. You can simply copy this form from the book.
6. After signing your contracts and turning the one in, we will assign you to your new Level 2 *Names of H.O.P.E.* small group with your small group leaders.
7. If you are not ready to get into a *Names of H.O.P.E.* small group, you are welcome to stay in the *Doorway to H.O.P.E.* group and repeat it. We would much prefer you to follow this plan than to stop joining us.
8. Finally, please take time to fill out the ***Doorway to H.O.P.E.* Evaluation Form** found at the end of this lesson. You can simply copy this form from the book. We greatly appreciate your feedback, so thank you for providing it.
9. Now, with your new small group, move to your assigned room for **Checking In**.

Checking In

Take a minute to review the **Guidelines for Checking In** found in Lesson 1.

Please use this time today to talk about anything you are comfortable with sharing. You can share what has been happening lately in your life or how you feel about what we just discussed. Regardless of the issue, focus on how you feel about it and how it is affecting you.

A good way to get started is by telling the people in your group about how you handled and answered the items from last week's **Acting on the Truth** section. Or maybe you might want to tell them if any of the items were particularly difficult to deal with or hard to understand. You may also tell them if any of the things we just discussed are difficult for you to understand or accept. In addition, we encourage you to share your decision and how you feel about advancing to Level 2.

At the completion of your time, we would like you to say, "I'm in" signifying that your time is completed. If you do not want to share this week, that is fine. But we still require you to at least say, "I'm in."

To help you get started, you may want to address the following statements and questions:

1. Briefly introduce yourself.
2. Why are you here and what expectations do you have from this ministry?
3. Have you been in a group like this before and what was it like?
4. How do you feel about being here?

Transforming Benefits

1. **Living a transformed life characterized by spiritual and emotional wholeness.** If you take the next step and stick to it, you can reap the benefits of living a life of spiritual and emotional wholeness. In addition, God promises to restore you and your situation when He says in Joel 2:25, "*Then I will make up to you for the years that the swarming locust has eaten...*" (NASV). If you do, you will not regret it.
2. **Blessed Assurance.** When you accept Christ and His finished work on the cross, you have the Blessed Assurance of your eternal life being secured. This assurance will help you gain a new perspective on your life here and now.
3. **All the help you will need.** Realizing that Jesus has already given us the ultimate help we need by His death on the cross will give you the confidence you need that He will also give you all the help you need to move forward and make healthy changes in your life.
4. **Continue transforming your mind by dwelling on God's truth.** By memorizing the scripture verses, you will begin filling your mind and heart with God's Truth. You are what you think. Proverbs 23:7 says, "*For as he thinks within himself, so he is*" (NASV). What we think about and dwell on will affect our feelings, which in turn affects our attitudes, which ultimately, affects our behavior. You can begin to transform all of these by spending increasing amounts of time thinking about truth. By memorizing and focusing on the truth in the verses that prove how you can experience wholeness and healing through Jesus Christ and His process of transformation, you can change how you think about your status in life in relation to your painful situation.

Contract for Membership in a *Names of H.O.P.E.* Small Group

I, ________________________________, do hereby agree to become a member of a *Names of H.O.P.E.* Small Group. I will give God the time to complete all the lessons in the book and be open to following His will and His plan for transforming my life and helping me overcome my painful experiences. During this time I will commit to:

1. Faithfully attending the group meetings.
2. Being an active participant in this program.
3. Honestly and diligently doing the homework in **Acting on the Truth**.
4. Being honest to myself and to God about my life and my pain.
5. Being open to making any changes God wants me to make.

This copy of your contract **is intended to be an agreement between you and God**. If you pledge to do this, please sign and date below and keep this contract in a place where you will see it regularly over the time it takes to complete all the lessons in the *Names of H.O.P.E.* book.

Thank you for choosing to continue on your journey through God's process of transformation. You will not regret it.

Signature: ____

Date: ____________________________

Contract for Membership in a *Names of H.O.P.E.* Small Group

I, __________________________________, do hereby agree to become a member of a *Names of H.O.P.E.* Small Group. I will give God the time to complete all the lessons in the book and be open to following His will and His plan for transforming my life and helping me overcome my painful experiences. During this time I will commit to:

1. Faithfully attending the group meetings.
2. Being an active participant in this program.
3. Honestly and diligently doing the homework in **Acting on the Truth**.
4. Being honest to myself and to God about my life and my pain.
5. Being open to making any changes God wants me to make.

This copy of your contract **is intended to be turned in to the H.O.P.E. leaders** so we know you are interested in being a member of the next *Names of H.O.P.E.* group. If you pledge to do this, please sign and date below and return it to one of the H.O.P.E. leaders.

Thank you for choosing to continue on your journey through God's process of transformation. You will not regret it.

Signature: ____

Date: ______________________________

Doorway to H.O.P.E. Evaluation Form

1. How did you first learn about this group?

   ____

2. What motivated you to attend?

   ____

3. What brought you back after the first meeting?

   ____

4. Were the meeting times too long? ___ Too short? ___ Right length? ___

5. If childcare was provided at your location, did you utilize it? Yes___ No___ N/A___

6. If childcare was not available, could you still attend? Yes___ No___ N/A___

7. Do you feel that the group provided a "safe" place for you to talk about your personal pain? Yes___ No___

8. Do you feel like we met our eight goals as they were explained to you in week one? Yes___ No___ If no, can you please explain why you feel we did not?

   ____

   ____

9. What would you tell someone who is considering attending H.O.P.E.?

   ____

10. As a result of your participation in the group, do you feel closer to God?___ Further from God?___ The same as you did before?____

11. As a result of your participation in the group, do you feel more hopeful?___ Less hopeful?___ The same as you did before?___

12. Complete this sentence: "The best thing that has happened to me as a result of my involvement in H.O.P.E. is: ____

    ____

13. H.O.P.E. could be improved if: ____

    ____

    ____

Appendix A: *H.O.P.E.* Guidelines

1. ***Safety.*** Our objective is to make our groups a place where we can feel safe to be vulnerable. Members will need to determine their own safety zones and what goes beyond those zones. The goal is to have everyone feel safe enough to expand those comfort zones as time elapses. If a discussion goes beyond a safety zone, the participant may excuse themselves from the group (just please let us know if you are only leaving for the week or for the remainder of the course).
2. ***Confidentiality.*** This is a necessity (except in a rare case where a person's safety and health is threatened and the responsible thing is to do otherwise. For example: threat of physical harm to self or others, child abuse or neglect, adult abuse, etc., plus issues that require consultation by the group leader with the other group leaders). We want everyone to feel free and safe to share his or her issues without the threat of ridicule, judgment or exposure.
    i. In the event of a breach of confidentiality, the responsible individual will be required to address the entire group and we will handle it in the group setting.
3. ***Acceptance.*** The basic principle that defines H.O.P.E. is that we are here to welcome anyone who comes to us for help. H.O.P.E. is not a social club, a private club or a clique. We are here to welcome everyone, along with their problems and pain.
    i. This means that we are very serious about not allowing any other agendas to develop within the ministry that conflict with our principles, goals, purpose, vision and guidelines. If you see or experience a problem in this area at any time that you are a member of one of our H.O.P.E. groups, please bring it to the attention of your group leader.
4. ***This is not therapy***. The leaders are not here for advice. As a transformation group, we are here to support, encourage and assist you on your journey through God's process of transformation. By sharing our stories we will gain strength as a group. But what is shared should not be interpreted as direct advice from the leaders of the group. If more intensive therapy is desired, we can refer you to individuals who can help you pursue that independently of this group.
5. ***Accountability.*** The participation and actions of all H.O.P.E. members are accountable to the other group members, leaders and the guidelines of H.O.P.E. H.O.P.E. is not a spectator sport and we will not enable those who seek our help to develop into spectators. Neither will we allow H.O.P.E. members to act in a manner that deviates from our purpose, principles or guidelines.
    i. For leadership accountability, we will not meet with group members of the opposite sex alone outside of the group. However, if needed, the leaders will make themselves available to group members by telephone, email or group meetings. (In all situations, a third party is highly recommended in meetings, on conference calls or copied on written communications). Plus, we highly encourage group members to meet in safe situations outside of the group and develop their support networks.
6. ***First person focus.*** When issues directly involve other parties, we will limit our remarks to those in the first person. We will not allow the "bashing" of others. We are not here to criticize, condemn or attack others; we are here to support you. It is important that the focus remains on you and therefore discussions that deviate from that will not be tolerated. During the time of **Checking In**, we also ask that you limit your remarks to 3-5 minutes in order to give everyone equal opportunity to share.
7. ***The person speaking during Checking In has the floor.*** When someone is Checking In, other group members are not to interrupt them. **Checking In** is to be free from disruptions, interruptions, criticism or judgmental comments. As long as the information you share is focused on how you feel about it or how it is affecting you (good, bad or ugly), we want to hear about it. What you share can be directly

related to a topic from the lessons, totally unrelated to the lesson topics and about something happening in your life right now, or somewhere in between.

i. If a member's Checking In gets "off track" or becomes inappropriate, it is the group leader's responsibility to direct them back on course. At the completion of a member's Checking In, if other group members want to share supportive and encouraging remarks, that is OK. In fact, we encourage it. Just remember Guideline 4 and that this is not therapy and those comments are not to be interpreted as professional advice.

8. ***Prayer.*** We would appreciate members praying for the other group members. This will be beneficial in providing the support network necessary for courage and renewed strength to take action on the road to transformation.

Appendix B: Contract for H.O.P.E. Leaders (Your Copy)

I, ________________________________, do hereby agree to become a H.O.P.E. leader. As a H.O.P.E leader (whether my role is a group leader or a leader within the organization), I will conduct myself in a manner consistent with the purpose, vision, principles and guidelines of H.O.P.E. I further agree to abide by and be accountable to all the responsibilities of a leader in H.O.P.E. as outlined in the **Guidelines for *Doorway to H.O.P.E.* Small Group Leaders**.

As a H.O.P.E. leader, I will also:

1. Support the efforts of H.O.P.E. in a manner consistent with my position.
2. Be open to following God's plan and purpose for my own life as I continue on my own journey through God's process of transformation.
3. Faithfully attend the group/organization meetings and functions applicable to my position.
4. Cultivate and promote the value of spiritual and emotional health from a Biblical perspective.

I understand that failure to fulfill the responsibility of my position or abide by the purpose, vision, principles and guidelines of H.O.P.E may result in removal from my position in H.O.P.E. if failure to comply/abide continues. I understand that I may also resign from my position if I desire.

This copy of your contract **is intended to be an agreement between you and God.** If you agree with and pledge to this, please sign below and keep it where you will see it often.

Thank you for choosing to serve with H.O.P.E. We greatly appreciate you and your decision.

Signature: ________________________________

Date: ________________________________

Printed Name: ________________________________

Address: ________________________________

City, State, Zip: ________________________________

Home Number: ________________________________

Cell Number: ________________________________

Email address: ________________________________

Appendix B: Contract for H.O.P.E. Leaders - Continued (Our Copy)

I, ______________________________, do hereby agree to become a H.O.P.E. leader. As a H.O.P.E leader (whether my role is a group leader or a leader within the organization), I will conduct myself in a manner consistent with the purpose, vision, principles and guidelines of H.O.P.E. I further agree to abide by and be accountable to all the responsibilities of a leader in H.O.P.E. as outlined in the **Guidelines for *Doorway to H.O.P.E.* Small Group Leaders**.

As a H.O.P.E. leader, I will also:

1. Support the efforts of H.O.P.E. in a manner consistent with my position.
2. Be open to following God's plan and purpose for my own life as I continue on my own journey through God's process of transformation.
3. Faithfully attend the group/organization meetings and functions applicable to my position.
4. Cultivate and promote the value of spiritual and emotional health from a Biblical perspective.

I understand that failure to fulfill the responsibility of my position or abide by the purpose, vision, principles and guidelines of H.O.P.E may result in removal from my position in H.O.P.E. if failure to comply/abide continues. I understand that I may also resign from my position if I desire.

This copy of your contract **<u>should be submitted to the leader of your H.O.P.E. location.</u>** If you agree with and pledge to this, please sign below and submit it to your H.O.P.E. leader.

Thank you for choosing to serve with H.O.P.E. We greatly appreciate you and your decision.

Signature: ______________________________

Date: ______________________________

Printed Name: ______________________________

Address: ______________________________

City, State, Zip: ______________________________

Home Number: ______________________________

Cell Number: ______________________________

Email address: ______________________________

Appendix C: Checklist for Entry into a Level 2 *Names of H.O.P.E.* Small Group

1. Group Member's Name: ______________________________

2. Has the member been regularly attending the *Doorway to H.O.P.E.* group (and have they attended a majority of the lessons)? Yes No

3. Have they been participating in the *Doorway to H.O.P.E.* group/lessons? Yes No

4. Have they been doing the homework in the **Acting on the Truth** section of the *Doorway to H.O.P.E.* lessons? Yes No

5. Have they been expressing their feelings during the **Checking In** portion of the *Doorway to H.O.P.E.* group? Yes No

6. Are they open and honest about their pain and problems? Yes No

7. Have they acknowledged their need for Christ and looking to trust Him for help? Yes No

8. Are they serious about making healthy changes in their life and open to allowing God to transform them? Yes No

9. Have they been adhering to ***all*** of the H.O.P.E. Guidelines? Yes No

10. Have they been accepting of and accountable to others in the group? Yes No

11. Are they compliant with the purpose, vision, guidelines and principles of H.O.P.E.? Yes No

12. Are they being supportive (and not critical, condemning or judgmental) of others in the group? Yes No

13. Did they sign their contracts for the *Doorway to H.O.P.E.* and *Names of H.O.P.E.* groups? Yes No

14. Do the *Doorway to H.O.P.E.* group leaders feel they are ready for a Level 2 *Names of H.O.P.E.* group? Yes No

15. Have the *Doorway to H.O.P.E.* group leaders been able to answer "Yes" to all (or a vast majority) of these questions? Yes No
    a. If "Yes", then the group member is ***likely ready*** to join a Level 2 *Names of H.O.P.E.* small group and they should be highly encouraged to do so.
    b. If "No", (or if any critical areas remain in doubt) then the group member is ***likely not ready*** to join a Level 2 *Names of H.O.P.E.* small group. In this case, the group member should be encouraged to go through the *Doorway to H.O.P.E.* group again.

   i. However, at this point the group member needs to be reminded of the H.O.P.E. accountability guideline (guideline number 5). Make certain they understand that H.O.P.E. is not a spectator sport and we will not enable those who come to us to develop into a spectator.
   ii. The same scenario applies for any behavior from a member that falls outside of our principles and guidelines.

c. If "No" and the group member has already gone through the *Doorway to H.O.P.E.* group twice (or possibly three times if an exception to this guideline was warranted), then it is recommended that the group member ***not*** be placed into a *Names of H.O.P.E.* small group.
   i. Once again, H.O.P.E. is not a spectator sport and we will not enable those who come to us to develop into spectators. Therefore, if someone has only been acting as a spectator to this point (having already gone through the *Doorway to H.O.P.E.* group two or possibly three times), they will most likely not take the Level 2 group seriously. This will most likely have a negative effect on the Level 2 group, which is exactly what we try to avoid because it is unfair to the other group members. Therefore, use the appropriate caution and discretion with proceeding with such a group member. You may have to inform such a group member that unless they change, they will not be able to continue on through our program.
   ii. The same scenario applies for any behavior from a member that falls outside of our principles and guidelines.

Printed in the United States
By Bookmasters

24 HEART-FELT SONGS OF PRAISE

Music From The Heart Of God

HYMNAL I

DORIS WESLEY- BETTIS

Scripture taken from the King James Version of the Bible.

This book is a work of non-fiction. Unless otherwise noted, the author and the publisher make no explicit guarantees as to the accuracy of the information contained in this book and in some cases, names of people and places have been altered to protect their privacy.

WestBow Press books may be ordered through booksellers or by contacting:

WestBow Press
A Division of Thomas Nelson & Zondervan
1663 Liberty Drive
Bloomington, IN 47403
www.westbowpress.com
1 (866) 928-1240

ISBN: 978-1-5127-3905-3 (sc)
ISBN: 978-1-5127-3906-0 (e)

Library of Congress Control Number: 2016906612

Print information available on the last page.

WestBow Press rev. date: 4/26/2016

TO

Yvonne Reed Matthews

Contents

Foreword

God has always had his hand on my life. I can remember as a child having a sensitive heart to the things of God. I remember reading bibles and reference books that my mom had lying around the house. I can still picture some of those things in my mind today.

I also remember the great faith my mother had when she was challenged by many things in her life. My mom prayed a lot; she went to the saints' houses for prayer, seeking more of God answers to prayers that were pending. Many times I was right there with her. I was the one who went to church with her during the mid-week services, and often had to sit patiently until she was done talking. I saw God answer her prayers. Years later, my dad gave his life to Christ, as well as, her five children.

One day, church and prayer would have an effect on me as well; in fact, for the rest of my life. I thank God for those holy things of God that were planted and rooted in me through prayer and the Word of God. I treasure my Apostolic foundation today.

I will never forget having my own prayer time with God as a child. On one occasion, my mom lost her keys and could not find them. She was desperately looking for them because they were the only set she had. So, she made an offer for help, and there was a twenty-five cents reward to whomever found them. I prayed to God to help me find them and I did. That's when I began to believe in God and talk to him. I was about six years old.

From that point on, God began to give me gifts: sewing by hand, singing, drawing; then around ten years old, I started writing songs that were secular. By the age of twenty-one, God saved me and I heard a message from the late Bishop G.W. Ayers about the "Buried Talents." The message stayed with me all night. It was then that I asked God to renew my gift of writing, only for him. From that day until now, the flow of songs has never stopped.

The first song That God gave me was: "Lord, Help Me Fight This Battle." Shortly after that, God gave me a song called, "He Made a Way for Me." I sang it one day from the choir stand during testimony service. It took the attention of the whole church. I knew from that moment on that's what God wanted me to do, write and sing them. Then, God started giving me choir songs that I couldn't sing by myself, so I formed a singing group as an outlet. It was short lived, but I continued to get even greater songs that needed a larger platform. God gave an invitation through Mrs. Yvonne Reed Matthews in 1985 to present two songs of mine in a local church workshop. I was so humbled by this that I did. The following year God gave me "Gospel Uplift Workshop" as an avenue to present this anointed music of God. It was a success for fifteen years, mainly under the direction of Yvonne Matthews and Bunny Jones.

God has given me traditional, as well as, contemporary gospel music. I have anthems, as well as, hymns. Today I am so honored to share them with the world. These songs contain the Word of God. I give them as God has given them to me. I read once in a reference book that, "Songs are a good way to remember the word of God." It's the song that ushers in the presence of the Lord during a church service. It is the song that lifts spirits when they are broken and in deep despair. It's a song that contains the Word of God that can pull men from the pits of hell.

My song, ***"Stop By Lord, Stop By"*** that is featured in this book, has been recorded by Dr. James Abbington of GIA; it has been taught at Emory University, Atlanta, Georgia; and is featured on YouTube by several youth and adult choirs across the United States and abroad. Also, in this book is the song, "New Heaven," sung by the New Jerusalem Fire Choir of Israel. Others have been used in workshops, on albums, documentaries, and are now featured in this book, ***"Music From The Heart Of God."***

I pray and hope that the songs in this book will be a blessing in lives everywhere. I pray that they will minister to the needs of God's people. Amen.

Thanks

God has allowed me once again to put his thoughts on paper. These songs are precious to me as well as God. I have been writing gospel songs for over forty years. It has been a blessed, God-given opportunity and honor to write these messages of God. Thank you Lord! It has been a pleasure to serve and minister in this calling.

I have never taken this gifting lightly; that is why we are where we are today, meaning: God, Yvonne and I. Yvonne, I simply say thank you, for it has been well over thirty years that we have come together in workshops, city choirs, and churches to present this awesome work of God. I only hear them. You bring them to life so that others may share in the joy, and that God may receive the glory. When I couldn't take them, you carried them. When I was trying to polish them, you made them shine. Thank you for scoring and re-scoring each song to make them as professional as can be. Thank you for your unselfish commitment to help me finish this work, ***"Music From The Heart Of God."***

They've gone across these United States, South America, and abroad because you too heard the voice of God concerning me. He must have told you to help me and you did. Yvonne, thanks!

I thank God for my husband of over 20 years, Richard T. Bettis, who learned how to play my songs by ear. We have ministered many times to the people of God. God knew what he was doing when he gave me you. You saw all the agony and pain it took to get this work out. You helped me push out the vision God had placed inside of me. For your dedication, patience and love, I thank you. But, we yet have more work to do for God's kingdom.

Minister Bunny Jones, thanks for using your gifts for the glory of God. Your anointed singing and directing made songs like "Well Done," "New Heaven," and "God is Going To Move Your Mountain" come to life. Special thanks to ministers Mark Finley, S. O'Neal Porter, Michael McCants, and David Fairley for your continued support down through the years. Thanks for your prayers Minister Claudette Prince and Mrs. Shirley Scott. I love you all.

A Mansion Not Made By Hands

II Corinthians 5:1

Doris Wesley Bettis

18
1.
glo ry glo ry glo ry hal-le lu - jah Hear the an-gels sing I'm look-ing for a
22
2.
B
Soloist
(sing)
For we know if this earth-ly house of this tab-er-na-cle were dis- solved
25
We have a buil-ding of God a house not made with hands It's e - ter nal in the hea- vens
28
C
Choir with Solo ad libs
It's e-ter-nal in the hea-vens I'll be glad when I get there I hope that you will be there

32
be there when they crown Him Lord of lords I hope that you will be there
36
be there when they march a round God's throne Don't tell me that I can't go I
40
D
can't go You can't hin-der me O sing-ing glo-ry glo-ry glo-ry hal-le
44
1.2.
3.
ritardando
lu - jah O sing-ing lu - jah Hear the an-gels sing

ARE YOU STANDING ON A ROCK

12
So - lid Rock Je-sus Christ that So - lid Rock Je-sus Christ is that So - lid
17
Soloist
B
Rock
If the ground that you're stand-ing on is but sink-ing sand then you
8vb
(8)
21
need to stand on Je sus for He will and I know He can If you're stand-ing on a rock that will
24
ne-ver give - a way Je-sus Christ is the So - lid Rock Je-sus Christ is the

28
Choir
So - lid Rock Je- sus-Christ is the So - lid Rock - - - I am

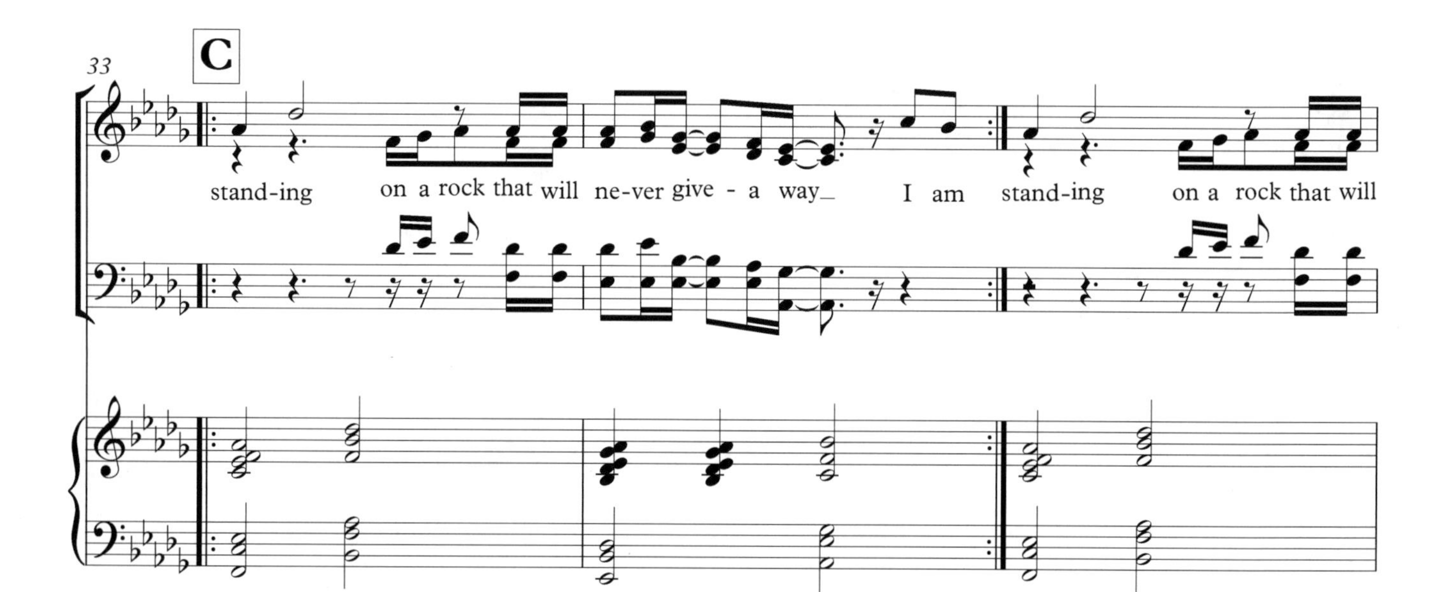
33
C
stand-ing on a rock that will ne-ver give - a way_ I am stand-ing on a rock that will

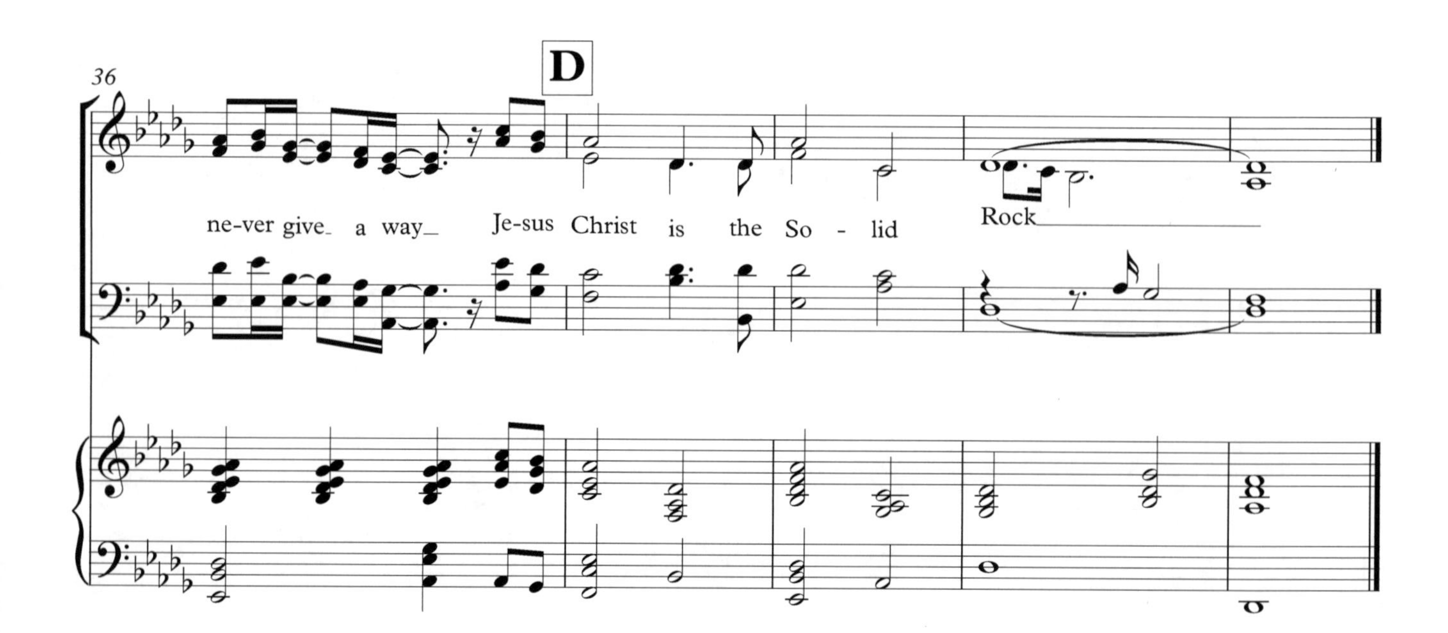
36
D
ne-ver give_ a way_ Je-sus Christ is the So - lid Rock

BY THY BLOOD

Doris Wesley Bettis

18
C
slain and hast redeemed us to God By Thy blood By Thy blood E' vry kin dred - and e'-vry

23
D
tongue E'-vry peo-ple and e'-vry na- tion - - For Thou wast slain and hast re-

27
1.
deemed us to God By Thy blood By Thy blood For Thou wast

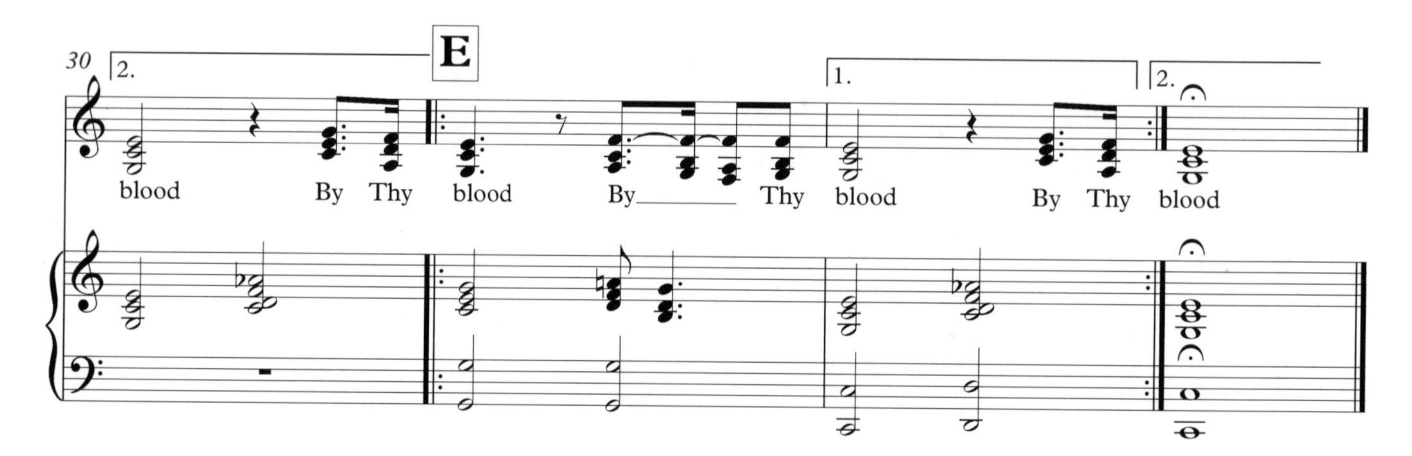
30
2.
E
1.
2.
blood By Thy blood By Thy blood By Thy blood

DIDN'T HE MAKE A WAY

Doris Wesley Bettis

had me bound I was lost but_ now___ I'm found Since Je - sus came and de li - vered me
my__ face My God o-pens a noth - ther place The Word of God says_ He's__ the Way
Choir
C
Now I stand in___ lib - er - ty When the e-ne-my said, "No way" Je - sus said, "I
I know for sure He's the on-ly Way
1.
To A(Verse1)
D
Solo ad libs
2.
am the Way" Didn't He Didn't__ He make a way___
Didn't He
E
F
Didn't He Didn't__ He make a way___
He made a way

G
He made a way
He made a way
He made a way
H
When the e - ne - my said, "No way"
Je - sus said, "I
am the Way"
Didn't He Didn't He make a way

GOD IS GOING TO MOVE YOUR MOUNTAIN

Doris Wesley Bettis

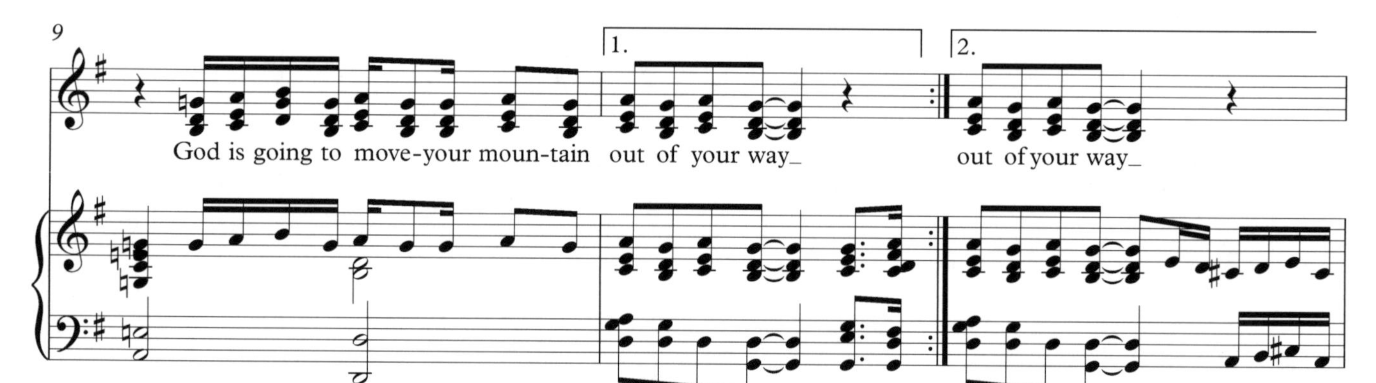

17
car-ry us from here to a-no-ther day
out of your way
21
It may be death or sor row
It may seem the pain won't go a- way
25
D. S. al Coda
But you can move e-v'ry moun_tain just with the words you say
29
rit.
God is going to move
God is going to move-your moun-tain out of your way
rit.

GOD IS GREAT INSIDE OF ME

Doris Wesley Bettis

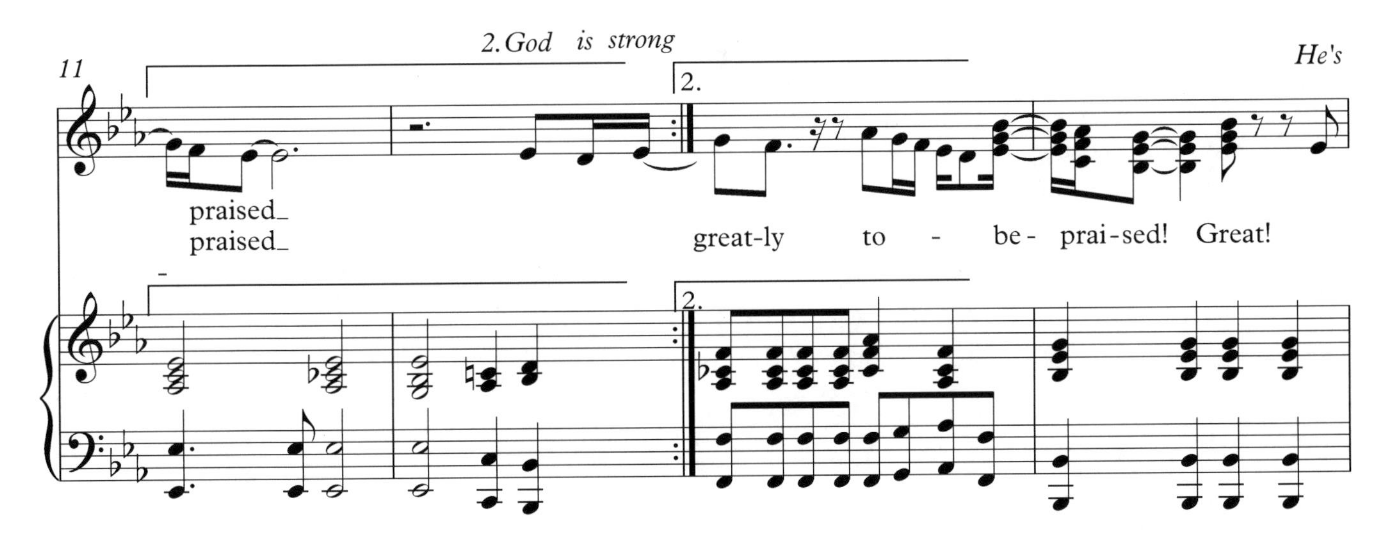
11
2. God is strong
He's
2.
praised_
praised_
great-ly to - be- prai-sed! Great!
2.

B
1.2.
3.
great! He's great! He's great_ He's great_ God is great
Great! Great! Great! Great!
B
1.2.
3.

C
rit.
God is great and He's great-ly to - be - praised_
C

GOD IS REAL TO ME